AFTER IMAGES

Also by Kingsley Tufts

POEMS: New and Collected *1983*
THE MYSTERY OF POETRY *1983*
PICO STREET STORIES *1984*
THERE'S A CRACK IN MY MARTINI *1984*
SHORT STORIES *1984*
THE LITTLE WHITE SONG BOOK FOR PEACE *1984*
THE WONDER OF THINGS *1984*
IMAGES AND PERCEPTIONS *1984*
CONCEPTS AND IMPRESSIONS *1989*
FRAGMENTS AND CONSEQUENCES *1990*
FORM AND ESSENCE *1993*

AFTER IMAGES

THE COLLECTED POEMS OF

KINGSLEY TUFTS

Fithian Press / John Daniel and Company
Santa Barbara, 1994

PRINTED IN THE UNITED STATES OF AMERICA

PUBLISHED BY FITHIAN PRESS / JOHN DANIEL AND COMPANY
A DIVISION OF DANIEL AND DANIEL, PUBLISHERS, INC.
POST OFFICE BOX 1525
SANTA BARBARA, CA 93102

LIBRARY OF CONGRESS CATALOGING-IN-PUBLICATION DATA
Tufts, Kingsley
After images: the collected poems of Kingsley Tufts / Kingsley Tufts.
p. cm.
ISBN 1-56474-084-6
I. Title.
PS3570.U38A17 1994
811'.54—dc20 93-33523
CIP

ACKNOWLEDGEMENTS

Many of these poems first appeared in *American Fireside* (formerly *Verseland*), *The American Mercury, The American Scholar, The Bard, Better Verse, Blue Moon, The Bookmaker's Folio, Carillon, Caravan, Children of the Sun, The Circle, Contemporary American Men Poets, Coronet, Cycle, Esquire, The Gypsy, Harper's Magazine, Kaleidograph, The Ladies' Home Journal, The Lantern, Let Us Sing, Literature, Muse, The New Yorker, Poet Lore, Poetry Caravan, Poetry World, The Quickening Seed, Shards, Silhouettes, Verse Craft,* and *The Washington Post.*

Many of these poems have been anthologized in *The Caravan of Verse, The Century Anthology of Verse, From a urving Bowl, Moon in the Steeple, Outstanding American len Poets: 1938, The Paebar Anthology of Verse, The Bard, thology of Magazine Verse and Yearbook of American try, Harper's Magazine, The Poetry Digest Annual hology of Verse, The Poetry House Anthology, Sparks Afar, This Is My America.*

M
A
Po
An
and

CONTENTS

AFTER IMAGES

LOVE

KATHLEEN

I love you as the morning sun
Loves the meadow, gold and green,
As moonlight loves when white clouds run
Above the hills; my love, Kathleen
Is like the softest touch between
Two wings, two seeds, two stones; I mean

I love you as the thin night rain
Loves the dust that's warm and dry,
As lightning loves the far refrain
Of thunder in a summer sky,
As fireflies love the dark, so I
Love you. And when I die

I'll love you as the faintest breeze
Loves white sails and outspread wings;
As rainbows touch the wet-leafed trees
I'll touch your world. In all these things
That cannot last—in all such things—
I'll be the part that cries, that sings.

DOWN THE HILL TOGETHER

Let's run down the hill together,
Fly like flags in windy weather;
There's a spring will quench our thirst—
Race, to see who gets there first!

Breathless, down the sun-swept hill,
Breathing deep, we'll drink our fill
Kneeling in a shady place,
Dripping, laughing, face to face.

Lovely weather, lovely wind!
Coats unbuttoned, hair unpinned!
Downhill to the spring we fly,
Heart to heart, my love and I.

TOGETHERNESS

The kite against the blue
    The sail against the sea
By cord and mast are held
    As you hold me.

The stone deep in the earth
    All the eons through
Is not more surely held
    Than I hold you.

Until the seas are empty
    And winds have died away,
Until the earth stops turning
    Our love will stay.

As masted sail we've fared,
    As corded kite we've flown,
As earth and stone are we
    By love alone.

PROMISE

Think only this while weeping
    If we must part;
I gave into your keeping
    Dear, my heart.

Though blackest night should cover
    All things ill
And no brave wind pass over
    An earthly hill

Though stars be cold above you
    And angels lonely,
Still I am near and love you,
    Love you only.

WARMTH

Memoried in my flesh and bone
    To keep me from the cold
Is all the earthly warmth I've known
    And all my heart can hold.

I've shared with ocean wind and wave
    The deep warmth of the sun,
Felt warmth of firelight in the cave
    Of night when day was done.

I've lain with love and known the bliss
    That only lovers know—
The warmth of soul and body kiss
    And morning's afterglow.

Nature's arms and arms of love
    Have warmed me through and through—
How blest I've been by heaven above,
    By sun and fire and you.

CATCH-UP

"You can't catch me," my true love said,
    "I'm changing much too fast.
You only catch the way I've been
    In flickers of the past.

"If I should stop, you might catch up
    But that would never do,
For then you'd have the only me
    And that would bother you.

"I'll never quite be caught by you
    Or you be caught by me
And that's the way love is, my dear—
    A catch-up mystery."

WINGS NEAR A FOUNTAIN

Swerving through sunlight, she parts from her own;
Into the rainbow the wind has blown,
Down to her fountain she flies alone.

Leaping and laughing, the clear water flows;
The touch of its music she loves, she knows.
Afloat in the pool of it, petals of rose.

You, too, have a fountain to which you go
Where the murmur of laughter is soft and low.
You swerve in the sunlight; you think I don't know.

Down through the rainbow swiftly you fly;
Your wings make a shadow where rose petals lie.
I'm glad that you go there; I'll never ask why.

YOU

Perhaps upon the street I might have passed you,
But I didn't;
At the door I seemed to feel you would be waiting,
But you were not;
Inside I half expected there to find you,
But the room was quite the same as I had left it.

Will I ever know what life, and you, and I
Could mean within a lovely room together?
Or must I seek forever without finding,
And never touch the real, the living you?

Must we always be so free?
How can it be
That I must go beyond all else to find you
And you can only be here when I'm gone?

ALL I COULD NOT SAY

Hear, when you hear this voice, Belovéd,
    These words of mine,
This stumbling phrase, this clouded thought,
    This halting line,
Hear, when the faltering cadence fails,
    Only the tone—
The resonance of all I could not say
    In words alone.

UPON THE WIND

You are my song, my golden wing,
    In fair and stormy weather;
With you I fly, with you I sing,
    Near to your heart, a feather.

So little is the warmth I bring,
    Yet as we soar together,
Gently, to your breast I cling,
    Against the wind, a feather.

OUR OTHER SELF

Together we are more than two
    Yet less than three;
Cool logic somehow glides askew
    When you're with me.

Some other self, and quite bizarre,
    Like dreams in sleep,
Makes more of us than what we are
    Alone, down deep.

It seems to be a self we share,
    But off and on;
Together, it is always there—
    Apart, it's gone.

NIGHT SONGS

Upon the pillowed darkness of the night
I end the day as one puts out a light.
Ah, what a wealth of love lies down with me—
What vagrant, fragrant wisps of reverie!

Sleep's avalanche slips slowly from above
On snowy chasms, melting, warmed with love,
And I am singing with the crystalled flow
Night songs I must have sung long, long ago.

I feel at last I am where I belong
With all my wealth of love and love of song—
A soundless singer till the night is gone,
Like melting snow, before the crush of dawn.

THE SHADOW MAN

At a sunlit fountain two children met
    Who were never to say goodbye,
And they splashed each other's faces wet,
    Without quite knowing why.

At a lovely fountain two children small
    Dropped pebbles over the brim,
And the little boy laughed when the sunlight's fall
    Made a shadow man of him.

And the little girl smiled when a certain cloud
    Sailed into the pool of blue;
Her eyes grew wistful, she turned very proud
    As a girl with a yacht might do.

Now where she has sailed to nobody knows;
    The fountain is empty and dry,
But the shadow man sometimes comes and goes
    As a stranger passes by.

NOT ONE, BUT THREE

My love, you are not one, but three—
The first is just the you I see;
The second is the one you'd be
In terms of biochemistry;
The third is all you are to me
In deepest felt reality.

And yet there may be more—a few
Illusions neither false nor true
That have a real persistence through
So many things you say and do—
Rare sleights of soul forever new
That mystify my love for you.

TRY TO REMEMBER

There were places, surely—
　　Just a few—
When you felt deeply, purely
　　You were you.

Were there moments, fleeting
　　As sparked stone
When the dearest heart beating
　　Was your own?

Try to think intently—
　　Before we met—
Love changes us so gently
　　We forget.

POPCORN CHILD

I sometimes think
    That I was born
Quick as a wink
    Like popping corn.

A popcorn child
    Heaven loaded
Hot and wild
    I just exploded.

From kerneled heart
    My self and soul
Were blown apart
    To popcorn bowl.

My soul sailed fair
    Across the blue
My self I share
    With salt and you.

SHARING AN ORANGE

Sharing an orange
Enraptured this little while
Urgency dissolves
In formless mist
Seeking the lost lotus
More intimate than love.

We kiss again
Asleep to seeds and rind
Desireless as death
In the sweet kissed orangeness
Upon our breath.

SILENT LOVE

We've grown too old with words, my dear,
Some sweeter than the songs of birds,
Soft spoken words, love telling words
Our foolish hearts cried out to hear.

Secret, sweetheart words, my dear,
Sex perfumed words, new married talk,
Bedroom, barnyard, sidewalk talk,
All love words, gentle and sincere.

So very many words, my dear,
To put our foolish fears to rest,
But silent love is still the best
When we are near, so very near.

PERFUME

I give you all the flowers whose fragrant kiss
Was ever on the wind or filled a room
Through nights of love and tender touching bliss.
I give you all the flowers whose fragrant kiss
Has ever filled love's longing deep abyss
With nearness in the darkness as they bloom.
I give you all the flowers whose fragrant kiss
Was ever on the wind or filled a room.

HARBOR SONG

I'll not put out this morning,
    There's a storm upon the sea;
My nets have need of mending, aye,
    And you have need of me.

I dare not risk good fortune;
    It'll blow the whole day through;
My nets have need of mending, aye,
    And I have need of you.

We'll tie the twine together,
    And listen to the rain;
We'll have a drop of whiskey, aye,
    And tie the twine again.

But I'll put out tomorrow,
    Nor worry anymore
With nets so strongly mended, aye,
    I'll haul the gold ashore.

WONDERING WHETHER

Are you now, or were you ever,
    Even in your fondest dream,
Quite as honest, quite as clever,
    Quite as loving as you seem?

With your arm about my shoulder,
    Why this little, nagging doubt?
Eyes may hoodwink the beholder—
    Some things rarely are found out.

As for me, not now or ever
    Will you get just what you see—
If I'm lucky, you will never
    Have these doubts of doubtful me.

CHRYSALIS HOUR

Ours for a night to laugh and to cry over
Something so frail as a flower-chain of clover;
Green like a green field the place of our weaving,
And fair what we wove—too fair for believing.

All through the night we watched with sweet aching
The white wings unfolding, the dark prison breaking.
How little we knew that the warm wind was drying
Those wings, while we watched, for the time of their flying.

Ours for a night, but the night now is over;
Broken the flower-chain we wove in the clover.
Up through the sunlight, on wings gently drifting,
The hour of our weaving, our dreaming, is lifting.

BODY AND SOUL

Today we go our way again, the same;
My hand in yours, our fingers intercurled.
You'll never know that last night while you slept
I helped to wash the garments of the world.

Today we go our way again, the same
Perhaps to you—perhaps less so to me;
For last night while you slept I traveled far
To kneel long hours and wash beside the sea.

SOMEDAY

You look at me, I look at you
  Uncertain where our future lies;
We look each other through and through,
  Reflected in each other's eyes.

Somewhere, in there, behind our faces
  In our bodies locked away
Are other loves and other places,
  Ghosts and ghouls of yesterday.

Someday they may walk in our eyes
  Concealed behind our lowered lashes,
Washed by silent tears that rise
  With disappointment's angry flashes.

My dear, they must not have their way;
  We'll live the bitter moment through—
We'll brush the silent tears away—
  You'll comfort me—I'll comfort you.

LOVE'S ARROW

Is there yet another way?
  So many ways I've tried
With all my might from day to day
  But now I can't decide
If I should just give up or try
  Once more for some way new—
Some perfect way to tell you why
  And just how much I love you.

Alone and gently, I shall start
  As I have done before—
To draw Love's arrow from my heart
  And polish it once more.
I only wish these lines might show
  The arrow flashing through
So brilliantly that you will know
  How very much I love you.

THE BEST MEDICINE

Laughter in the morning
    Does a body good—
It helps to ease the miseries
    The way that liquor should.

Laughter in the afternoon
    Makes the juices flow
That wash away the weariness
    Of worldly work and woe.

Laughter in the evening
    Soothes the nerves and mind—
It often dulls the dailyness
    That habit leaves behind.

Laughter after midnight
    When tiredness takes its toll
Not only balms all bitterness—
    It heals the heart and soul.

Blest are we past midnight
    When push comes to shove
Who laugh in warm togetherness
    With someone that we love.

WE SHALL BE BORN

My love with yours shall merge and blend
    As wings in flight are flown—
In harmony, we shall transcend
    The lonely all alone.
Our loves, as one, shall bear us on
    To where our hearts would go,
And when our wingéd way has gone
    Through azure ebb and flow,
We shall be born as metaphors
    And lovely similes
On fragrance of forevermores
    In flowered eternities.

CARELESS THOUGHT

I would I were a wanderer
    With heart and mind so free
That nothing in this whole wide world
    Would ever bother me.

I would that I might wander
    Wherever I might choose
With nothing I might want too much
    Or fear too much to lose.

With empty hands and pockets
    I'd go where fancy led me
And when my wandering was done
    On careless earth I'd bed me.

There I'd wait the careless wind
    To wander by and find me
And waft me on my wandering way
    With nothing left behind me.

But I am not a wanderer—
    My heart and mind are tied
To desk and pen and someone who
    Just asked me why I sighed.

UNDER GREEN LEAVES

New loves hold the old loves in their hearts
    As the flowering trees in spring
Hold dead branches in their breasts
    Where mockingbirds sing.

GRIEF

On whom shall I lavish the love
    Of my lonely heart
When my world that was only you
    Has fallen apart?

To what shall I turn when darkness
    Shadows my day,
And where shall I go when I seem
    To have lost my way?

I live in a strange world of echoes
    That call and call,
And I look into space where there
    Is nothing at all.

Yet this, too, I know will pass;
    I tell my heart
To be patient and wait until grief,
    Too, shall depart.

ALL THROUGH THE NIGHT

All through the night my fingers cry
    To touch a love lost long ago;
    It's quite impossible I know—
I know—I know—and that is why

My eyes are open wide and dry
    And though I keep my breathing slow
All through the night my fingers cry
    To touch a love lost long ago.

Midnight-morning hours go by,
    Outside the springtime warm winds blow;
    By lovers' bedsides soft lights glow—
I know—I know—and that is why
All through the night my fingers cry
    To touch a love lost long ago.

REGRET

Oh, how I wanted it all to be
So perfect just for you!
God must have cried upon the blue
When he made you and me.

With Him I cry, now that I see
Mischance my whole life through.
Oh, how I wanted it all to be
So perfect just for you!

I cry, my love—cry silently—
For all the good and true—
For all I hoped to be and do
The day you came to me.
Oh, how I wanted it all to be
So perfect just for you!

REVERIE

How safe it is, this living in the past,
Where all is as it was, where time stands still
Upon the sundial of my heart, its shadow cast
Across the hours my recollections fill.

It is so quiet, so secure from harm
In memory's garden always full in flower;
The sunlight holds me tenderly and warm
Against its breast, hour after quiet hour.

Here I am near to all the loves I knew
Before the autumn leaves began to fall;
Here in my garden there is always you—
The nearest and the dearest love of all.

Alone and peaceful, far from worldly care,
Dissolved in sunlight as the teardrops start,
I touch your face, caress your brow, your hair—
In reveries I hold you to my heart.

FLOWERS

I am you
    And when you look at me
With vision true
    It is yourself you see.

You and I
    Beneath the ground are one;
We live and die,
    We blossom and are done.

Side by side,
    Wild, brief-petaled flowers
We two abide
    The wind, the sun, the hours.

THE DOOR

To live from day to day
    Is hard to do
    As days grow few
And yearning goes astray
    In search of You.

To live from hour to hour
    Is harder still
    When weakened will
No longer has the power
    My hands to fill.

To live from breath to breath
    May easier be
    Perhaps I'll see
Beyond the edge of death
    You come to me

To take me through the door
    To take me far
    From star to star
At peace forevermore
    Where You are.

VALENTINE FLOWERS

If ever you grow tired of love
    Or love grows tired of you,
Remember roses, once so red,
    And violets, once so blue.

Remember when the stars above
    Were wishes that came true—
Remember all the things we said
    When love was fresh and new.

Remember, we were hand and glove
    In all that we went through—
Remember roses, once so red,
    And violets, once so blue.

THE GOLDEN YEARS

Through candlelight
    And crystal years
        Our love was warm and true;
Each tender night
Was silver bright
        At our table set for two.

Now plates are gold
    And gold the years
        Our memories golden too;
The hand I hold
Is wealth untold
        At our table set for two.

BEFORE NIGHT FALLS

Beyond the sunset let us softly go—
Long let us linger in the afterglow
    Before night falls.

Let us be silent as brief evening brings
The radiant glory of all lovely things
    The heart recalls.

Hushed with all the love that has been ours
Let us be quiet as the sleeping flowers
    On darkening walls.

Let us not leave but hand in hand stay on
Until the sunset afterglow is gone
    Before night falls.

REMEMBER

Remember the young years
    When only the loved things
        Were the ones we kept—
Those were the glad years
    When the heart had wings
        And the tears we wept
Were all for love, bright tears
    For the beautiful things
        Heaven y-clept.

Remember the sweet years
    When only the dear things
        Were the ones we kept—
For now in the sad years
    Love folds its wings
        And the tears wept
Are silent tears, love tears
    For the faltering things
        By Death y-clept.

OLD AS GRIEF IS THE SONG I SING

Old as grief is the song I sing,
Older than time with a black, crooked wing;
It was old when the world was a wee, crying thing
In a tattered gray blanket of stars.

When I sleep, when I wake, when I walk in the rain
It beats at my heart with a slow, dull pain
And it bids me return, with insistent refrain,
To the place where I first knew love.

Strange is the song as the song of the sea;
Full of unrest, and it seems to me
That something imprisoned cries to be free—
Something I know not of.

Old as the world is the song I sing,
And old is the sorrow a song may bring
When the years have crept under the black, crooked wing
And nothing remains that was ours.

RENDEZVOUS

I'll meet you tonight where the beetles sing
    In the wet weeds by the lake,
And we'll dance on a carpet of velvet scum
    By the light the fireflies make.

And you'll wear a crown as tall as the Queen's,
    Of pearls and tourmaline bars
That I filched from the treasure chest of night
    All diamonded with stars.

We'll dance to the music of whimsical worlds
    In the cat-tails close to shore,
Where tinkle the tiniest crystalline chimes
    That nobody hears anymore.

We'll dance all night, and tangle the world
    Criss-cross at all the turns;
Then steal away through the lush, cool leaves
    And hide among the ferns.

MY HAPPINESS

The fire burns low and chill voices
    Whisper through the night;
Gleaming eyes creep through the brush
    And watch the dying light.

But I feel you stir, and leave my side
    Careful I shall not wake.
You drag more branches to the fire;
    I hear them snap and break.

Up through the trees a shower of sparks
    Flames with an orange light,
And creeping things with gleaming eyes
    Steal back into the night.

EARTH SONG

Earth song,
Song of the builded nest
And the warm rain;
From feathered breast
To breast of mine
Swift flies the pain.

Quick fear,
And the slow fear clinging;
My love, come near!
Shall the song of my singing
Be lost on the wind
And you not hear?

Strong branch,
Branch of the strong oak tree
Where the prudent ones build,
Oh, mock not me
Who sing from the willow
Dreams unfulfilled.

BEDSIDE VASE OF BILLBERGIA

Persian teardrops, love beholding,
  Gently wept
  The night we slept
Each the other, holding, holding.

Teardrops still are falling, falling—
  Persian teardrops—
  How the heart stops
Near the dry vase, calling, calling.

WHEN LOVE GETS IN THE WAY

Whether you are old or young
    There's nothing you can say—
You can only bite your tongue
    When love gets in the way.

Whether you are rich or poor
    Until your dying day
There'll never be an open door
    When love gets in the way.

Whether you are weak or strong
    No man can say you nay
But you must stay where you belong
    When love gets in the way.

Whether this is good or bad—
    Be that as it may—
All you've got is what you've had
    When love gets in the way.

CHINA TEA

How lovely making love would be
If love and logic could agree;
    If consequences failed until
    None had to suffer or to kill,
How lovely making love would be!

With slow rain falling silently
And China's troubles far from me,
    With willows at the window sill,
How lovely making love would be!

Across the rice fields to the sea
The gulls are flying wild and free
    While I remain against my will
    Loyal to our country still,
Thinking, while I pour your tea,
How lovely making love would be!

COMMITMENT

Commitment unto death:
    The words bring tears
        And make my faint heart pound.
    Through all the years
        And all the world around
"Unto my dying breath,"
        Have been the words that sound
    The vow beyond all fears,
Even death.

Commitment unto you:
    My faith, my love,
        My friend, my native land—
    You will I place above
        All else—for you I stand
Steadfast, loyal and true.
        I give my oath, my hand,
    My life, that I might prove
This unto you.

LOVE AND LOYALTY

So interlaced are love and loyalty
The end of either, lost or broken free,
    In youth is tears and utter desolation,
    In age a sigh beyond all consolation
And to the Most Beloved a tragedy.

A sail forever parted from the sea,
A lock forever hasped without a key,
    These are the heart's despairing separation,
So interlaced are love and loyalty.

Beyond the breach there is no piety;
To friend and country no fidelity.
    Steadfast faith is more than obligation,
    Devotion more than safety or salvation.
Bond and breach embrace eternity,
So interlaced are love and loyalty.

OLD FRIENDS—OLD LOVES

We often wonder where they've gone—
The ones we knew before
We left them there and wandered on
To look for something more—
Another world—another dawn—
Another open door.

Perhaps they, too, have wandered far
From where we said goodbye
To follow some faint, distant star—
To find a bluer sky—
Perhaps they wonder where we are—
Remembering—wondering why—

Why the sad thoughts sometimes start
And memories that we carry
Rest so heavy on the heart
That otherwise were merry—
Why then it seemed so hard to part
And yet so necessary.

DISTANCE

I drink from distant wells and feel the fear
That death and distance are almost the same.
The nearest breath and touch, the whispered name
Reach from a distance; every sound I hear,
Song and heartbeat, bells, the Voice most dear
Are all remote; the distant flickering flame
Tells little of the Lamp from which it came;
I yearn to bring the far-away more near.

My heart begs always to embrace its love
And break the barrier of its separation,
Believing then its loneliness will cease.
My soul begs always that the heavens above
Will end the torment of its isolation,
Receiving it at last to rest in peace.

DOGS

Three brown dogs
Escapees
Drink at the fountain
Feel a hand stroking their chests
Rest
Return home.

Loneliness
Crossing the fountain brim
Caresses the still water
The heart
Parched with longing
Whispers a name.

YELLOW HIBISCUS

The yellow
Hibiscus
Warms
The ice-blue
Vase
Placed
Just there
Remembering.

TABLE FOR TWO

I shall never forget
As old as I get
There's nothing more charming
Intriguing, disarming
Than a girl at a table for two.
On my life I will bet
There will be nothing yet
More lovely, more rightful,
Seductive, delightful
Than to dine with a smiling
Amusing, beguiling
Girl at a table for two.

ROSES

Fresh roses
For a dead love
Fill the vase
That otherwise
Would hold nothing
Nothing at all.

The vase
Weeps crystal tears
The room
Empty as words
Before the fresh roses
Is emptier now.

BURNING

When love is gone
    The burning lingers
On and on
    In lips and fingers.

Joy of days
    Past all retrieving
Stays and stays
    In burning breathing.

Flesh enfolds
    All that was spoken
Holds and holds
    The true, the broken.

Flesh alone
    Is burning ember
Blood and bone
    Alone remember.

ETERNAL LOVE

There's love and love, and still again there's Love,
So there are sunsets, stars, and fresh sunrises,
No two the same below, between, above—
Each with its own chromatic quick surprises;
Each one the best until the mind surmises
Change must come as time's hard hand devises
Threats to all the heart is fondest of
Among a world of transient disguises.

Earth's glories all are only fleeting prizes
Lost the moment they are won, but Love
Defies the hand of time while time despises
Things that linger longest, and excises
All that would endure, tears off the guises,
Leaving Nature bare, but Love, true Love,
Time's worst offender, falters, falls and rises,
Laughs at change, and still is Love, is Love.

LOVE REMEMBERED

Remembrance of past love pervades each day
That brings reminders with the smallest things—
Black dates upon the calendars of time,
The street song of a radio that sings
An aria of the soul near the sublime—
A flame of love the city burns away.

Remembrance of past love we gently gave—
Asking only the beloved stay near
For proof that love would always be the same—
Recalls the heart with tenderness to hear
Love's vow once more, in memoried candle flame
As brief as time, as constant as the grave.

MY BLINDNESS

It has always been that way—you go with dreams
 While I must find my way as blind men do.
In the tremor of the earth my starlight gleams;
 Ofttimes I touch things still unseen by you.

A TRICK OF MEMORY

Long years ago and far away
 Parks and fountains, necklaced lights
Of bridges over mystic mirrors
 Thralled my days and nights.

Bewitched, I wandered in a haze
 Of golden windows, sunlit towers—
Green and orange and glowing red
 Were charming, changing flowers.

It was a strange, enchanted place—
 I hope it's still the same—
When I was there I was in love
 With—oh, dear! What's her name!

SPRINGTIME

Wild animals are mating,
 Wild birds are pairing up—
With fur and feathers waiting,
 The world's a loving cup.

No hand can paint the feeling
 That overtakes the lover—
That sends the senses reeling
 When the cup spills over.

Words fail the wondrous story
 Of ecstasy's sweet tryst
In wildwood glens of glory
 When the loving cup is kissed.

THREE KISSES

Hold out your hand, my darling one,
  And close your eyes for me;
I'll give you something fair and fine
  As ever you will see.

Three magic kisses in your palm
  To take with you to bed—
A pearl one white, a diamond bright,
  A ruby one that's red.

Now close your fingers very tight;
  Leave not one tiny crack.
With kisses, once they're really lost
  It's hard to get them back.

Quite soon a fairy Prince will come
  In robes of silvery blue,
And these three kisses in your palm
  Will make a queen of you.

FIRELIGHT

Firelight spoke
  Of memories,
Reminders of
  Such things as these:
The scent of leaf smoke
  On the breeze,
The burning notes
  Of symphonies,
And love.

SUSPICION

You just don't think I know, but you
Don't know I know and yet I do;
I just can't put my finger on
The voiceless lost, the touchless gone,
Nor can I name the hour or day
Like shedding hair it combed away.

But now I know I know I know
It's gone where all things lost must go—
Into some limbo, box or bin
That someone else's things are in.
I know, I know—my heart's aware—
It's gone—it could be anywhere.

You just don't think I know that we
Are not the way we used to be;
Perhaps it's nothing—just a chill,
A trampled grave—perhaps it will
Just pass away with morning light
If I lie silent one more night.

KISSES

Here's to them all: the peck, the brush,
    The flick, the cool intentional miss,
    The spiritual, the dry abyss,
The toothy press, the ripened mush!
    But oh, was ever one like this?
    Was ever one like this!
The fresh, strawberry juicy crush,
    The blushing, salivating bliss,
The heavenly rocket's hot blood rush
    Of youth and first love's clinging kiss!
    But oh, was ever one like this?
    Was ever one like this!

PREMEDITATION

How limiting it is
    To know what one is doing!
Cool premeditation
    Changes love to wooing.

When knowledge guides the hand
    And every act is willed,
The heart can feel neglected,
    Its longing unfulfilled.

There's something lost in knowing
    Too much when we adore,
And wooing is our sorrow
    If there is nothing more.

INITIATION

Billy, blow the candle out—
This is what it's all about;
Lay your hand upon my breast—
Love and I will do the rest.

Just forget that I am older—
Feel my hair caress your shoulder;
Hold me warm against your chest—
Love and I will do the rest.

Let my soft hands stray until
My lips have kissed you where they will;
Billy, do what you think best—
Love and I will do the rest.

GARDENIAS

The tears that fall
On rosaries
Are blesséd tears
But those
That fall on white
Gardenias are
The saddest tears
Love knows.

Gardenias call
Up memories
Of young years
Full of pain
The tears on white
Gardenias are
Deep soul tears
Cried again.

Old rainbows all
And reveries
In mists of tears
Depart
But tears on white
Gardenias are
The wounds, the spears,
The heart.

WHEN THEY SPEAK OF FIRST LOVE

They speak of it
Telling of something else
They cannot say
The unsayable
Whatever happened
Happened
To someone else
Who no longer
Exists.

The words belong
To strangers
Seeking
The unforgettable
Forgotten
The mystery
Of ancient waterfalls
Stilled by time
Gone with the sun.

THE FIRST TIME

The belly has no ear
    The heart no tongue—
We dared and felt no fear
    When we were young.

When such love had to stop—
    Now we are grown—
Our first time is a raindrop
    Laced in stone.

With sealed lips we mime—
    We must not say
Our first time was the last time
    We felt that way.

MEMORIES

The memories we accumulate
    With living day to day
Are often much too delicate
    To lightly talk away.

Some linger in the gossamer webs
    Of subtle secrecy
That keep the tender left-unsaids
    Of loves not meant to be.

Sometimes the void that lies between
    Maturity and youth
Looms darkly with the unforeseen
    Too dangerous for truth.

When reminiscence tempts the tongue
    To wag of life too much
Discretion hides the heart among
    The commonplace and such.

FORBEARANCE

A patient silence may betray
    Thoughts better never spoken;
Silence has its treacherous way
    Of sparing the unbroken.

But gentle bitterness that plays
    About the lips of someone
May hide far less than it conveys
    Of loving done and undone.

The heart too often disobeys
    In wordless quiet violence;
It bares itself in what it weighs
    On scales of patient silence.

WITH YOU

I found a poem not meant to preach—
I heard a song not meant to teach—
    And yet I learned a thing or two;
    I felt a thrill entirely new
From something far beyond my reach
    As when I walk and talk with you.

I wonder what it is that gives
The marvelous that lives and lives
    Beyond the touch of time and place,
    Beyond the poem, the song, the face,
That holds my heart—as fugitives
    Are held in freedom's sweet embrace.

With love and poetry and song
I am alive where I belong—
    With wind and eagle on the blue,
    With stars that shine the wild night through,
With all that's beautiful and strong—
    I am, I am—with you, with you.

WHAT I COULD NOT TELL YOU

You gave me love, yet kept yourself
    For yourself, as if to say
That love and you were never one,
    And it could be no other way.

You could not know that you and love
    For me, when all is said and done,
Were always, and will always stay,
    Flower and fragrance all in one.

PATHWAY OF DUST

Kind heart, true heart,
Love knows no ending;
Pure heart, dear heart
Love is transcending.
Rise on the white wings,
Fly through the dawn;
Fair are the far-lands
Calling you on.

Pause not, care not,
Love is unfearing;
Cry not, call not,
None shall be hearing.
Dead are the kind men,
Cold are the stones;
Raw are the sea winds
Bleaching their bones.

Kiss me, kiss me,
Who shall be knowing?
Your lips, my lips,
Where are we going?
High through the blue sky
Far, far away;
Love lifts the chalice,
Drink it today.

Kind love, true love,
Where are the far-lands?
Pure love, dear love
Black are the wet sands;
Tired are the white wings,
Love, let us part.
Cold is the sea weed
Clutching my heart.

THERE ARE DAYS

There are days
There are days
There are days and days
When I think of you
All the time.

And the tears I shed
On an empty bed
Flow tenderly
All the time.

The world goes around
And the radio plays
And I do what I do
In a haze
In a haze.

The world goes around
And around
And around
And the radio
Plays
And plays.

There are days
There are days
There are days and days
When I think of you
All the time.

FRUSTRATION

We planted it together, you and I,
And prayed in our hearts that it would live.

The loneliest hour of all my life, I think,
Was when it bloomed
And there was no one I could tell.

MADONNA

Sacred Virgin of Love,
Mother of Jesus,
How pale you are
In your place
On the wall
Looking down.

Do not smile!
Do not smile
That men have forgotten
The girl who was human,
A sweetheart, a darling,
Who lived in a small Jewish town.

ANONA

Anona, fair Anona, child of sorrow
Careless of today and of tomorrow,
  Here beneath Night's raven wing
  Loosen down your hair and sing
To the music of the waves along the strand.

Anona, fair Anona, pale and weeping,
Teardrops cannot hold within their keeping
  What the heart has locked within
  Of the dear things that have been—
They are only as the raindrops on the sand.

Anona, fair Anona, love forsaken
Only sleeps, more sweetly to awaken.
  Here beside the whispering shore
  Make a song of dreams once more
For the time when he again shall kiss your hand.

CHARADE

Dark and slender forms grotesque
    Weave upon the silver screen,
Rise and twine in blue burlesque
    As dancers dance unseen.

One shadow longer than the rest,
    Lithe and lovely, picturesque,
Slips from a flame within my breast;
    The flame of dreams on statuesque.

The gliding shadows quickly fade;
    Unseen, the dancers all depart,
The blue burlesque of love's charade
    Unfinished, dies upon my heart.

MOTHER

If thus the herald should sing from heights afar
    With clarion voice unto the heart of you:
    "Unbind your life from his, and say *adieu*;
The years are gone—forsake the double star
And henceforth be what in yourself you are
    Apart from him. To self alone be true
    For self is all!" Mother, what would you do?
How would you answer, being what you are?

The dreams of old that you gave up for me—
    Would you recall them now? Would you be glad
        For youth returned with all its glowing charms,
With things untried—your life gloriously free?
    Or would you smile at all you might have had,
        And choose again my face upon your arm?

CONSIDERING ALL THINGS

I wonder which is better, which is worse,
  To love the little things I love or spend
My tiny passion on a universe
  Too vast to hold or help or comprehend.

How safe they are—these easy things to love—
  The universe, humanity, the dream—
These lofty, empty words so far above
  The little things that hunger, kill and scream.

Yet must I love, as I have loved before—
  The brief, the broken and the torn apart;
My only need—were I to ask for more—
  A stronger stomach and a braver heart.

THE SEEDS OF YESTERDAY

The gardens all have vanished,
  Their glories passed away—
Oh, blesséd be the few who saved
  The seeds of yesterday.

In envelopes of memory,
  In jars love set apart,
Are stored the flowers and flavors
  Of gardens of the heart.

On shelves of time and trouble,
  In cellars sealed away,
Love's faith awaits the springtime
  In seeds of yesterday.

Oh, blesséd be the few who see
  Beyond death's wintry door
The empty gardens of the heart
  In flower and fruit once more.

BENEATH THIS LEAF

Beneath this fallen leaf the dust is dry—
    Only an autumn leaf, and yet enough
To turn a raindrop plunging from the sky—
    A brown leaf, and yet it was enough.

Though all our dreams, my dear, one day shall lie
    Beside this leaf, they'll be enough
To shield this pinch of dust that's you and I—
    One dream of all we've dreamed will be enough.

I WILL WALK BESIDE YOU

I will walk beside you when you are far from me;
You will feel my hand in yours wherever you may be.
        Walking on the starlit paths
        Beyond this earthly door
        You will feel that you and I
        Have walked them all before,
For we have known a magic love of charm and mystery.

As we have walked in deserts and strolled
    beside the sea,
Among all creatures great and small
    in perfect harmony,
        Where all things are familiar
        As they have been before,
I will walk beside you when you are far from me.

In golden light forever, two lovers such as we
Are pilgrims on a journey to a distant destiny.
        Hand in hand, we two will go
        As we have gone before,
        Enchanted to the end of time,
        Enraptured evermore.
With music and in fragrance, through all eternity,
I will walk beside you when you are far from me.

POETRY & THE ARTS

POETRY

Poetry is
Of Being:
Not sight alone
But seeing.

Poetry is
Never:
Words alone
Or clever.

Poetry is
This:
Not kiss alone
But bliss.

INSPIRATION

To give form to feeling—
    That's the thing!
Glorify the ceiling,
    Put wing
To sandals, spark to fingers,
    Sing, sing!
Bend iron, chip stone
Together! Alone!
    Ring, ring
With the bell ringers!
    Bring
Gifts of the Magi!
    Beautify
Man, earth and sky—
Every thing!
Give form to feeling—
    Try! Try!
Nothing concealing!
    That's the thing!
In God's name
    To Bring! Ring! Sing! Fly
With hearts aflame
    Before we die!

THE FENCE

I wonder, do you have a sense
  Of how I talk to you
Across the ink-and-paper fence
  That separates us two?

I wonder, do you read between
  The lines and feel each word
That tells the unseen I have seen,
  The unheard I have heard?

Though you are very near to me,
  Our worlds are far apart;
Across the fence I throw the key
  That has unlocked my heart.

I wonder, will the fence be there
  When I have had my say,
Or have I failed somehow, somewhere,
  And thrown the key away?

SUPPLICATION

I would to God some inner power divine
  Might find its way to shape itself in me
As tendrils shape upon the groping vine
  And rivers wind that seek the distant sea.

I would to God that I might feel some day
  The sphering of the raindrop falling far,
The conch's slow spiral searching out its way,
  The snowflake reaching for its crystalled star.

I would to God that I might feel in me
  Mine own making, that I might touch the spark
That smolders in the ash of destiny—
  That kindles all creation in the dark.

THE TRULY GREAT

From Potter's wheel a few great souls are spun
    More perfect than the rest, a few who reach
    The pinnacles of spirit, a few who breach
The barriers of the mind, the great undone.
Fine vessels fashioned by a power sublime
    They bear the best to which our lives aspire;
    Created from earth's clay and heaven's fire
They rest in glory on the shelves of time.

Protect them well! The least of us will fall
    Beneath a shattering blow—the vandal's test;
    Let no man break the beauty of the best!
The workmanship that made them made us all.
Flawed with doubt and envy though we be,
We owe this debt to God and pottery.

STYLE

How shall we write just what we mean
    With slippery-slidey symbols
When truth flows over and between
    Its measurements in thimbles?
We reach for truth with every word
    That seems to have acuity,
Yet every word that's read or heard
    Is tinged with ambiguity.
In vain our stylus makes its mark
    With speech and thoughts remembered;
Deletions and erasures spark
    Brief fire in script dismembered.

Yet all we mean is what we are
    In concept and impression—
With every symbol, scratch and scar
    Our soul kneels in confession.
The tear-stained tablet we retrace
    With stet and superceding
Is truth itself with waxen face
    Stylus pierced and bleeding.

THE QUEEN OF MEANING

Queen of every name and noun,
Sparkling diamonds in her crown,
    She comes to me alone
In her golden threaded gown
Oh, so gently stepping down
    In radiance from her throne.

Diamond facets flashing flame
In every language, every name,
    Illuminate her face.
Golden threads, no two the same,
From the brocade weaver's frame
    Embrace and interlace.

She comes as one who understands,
With smiling lips and outstretched hands,
    To offer me her crown—
To share with me her wonderlands—
With me, the least whom she commands—
    Her juggler, lover, clown.

THE ELEPHANT

Why an elephant in a basket?
    Why such weight in verse so fragile?
Friend and critic well might ask it—
Why an elephant in a basket?
Frail butterfly in leaden casket
    Might have far more grace and style.
Why an elephant in a basket?
    Why such weight in verse so fragile?

THE STING

Each word
A tiny mirror
Bent
To symbolize
The meant.

Each line
A chain
Of dangled lies
Bedazzling
The eyes.

Each verse
A trick
Designed
To mesmerize
The mind.

Each poem
A con
Of crafty art
To victimize
The heart.

THE TRUTH IS

If artists were creatures
    Autogenous
Produced by means quite
    Endogenous
Their works might be less
    Pathogenous
More truly divinely
    Pyrogenous
Narcissistic and auto
    Androgynous.

ART

Art of the mind
    And Art of the heart
Must dwell together
    Never apart.

The one goes mad
    When left alone;
Alone, the other
    Is fleshless bone.

The mind's design
    And the heart's cry
Need one another
    To satisfy.

RESOLUTION

I'll use the old words gladly
    In a plain and natural way
And hope I've not said badly
    The things I meant to say.

I'll ring old bells discreetly
    And love them all the more
If I have rung them sweetly
    As they've been rung before.

I'll tread old paths of duty
    That wiser men have trod;
I'll tell again the beauty
    Of the oldest gifts of God.

I'll use my pen as purely
    And as simply as I can;
For this I'll live obscurely
    As a poet and a man.

THEY ARE TWICE BLESSED

Blesséd above all others
Are they who find
Self fragments
In music
Art
Poems
In the remains
Of the makers
Who build civilizations
Of hopes and heartaches
Yearnings
Poignancies
Of body and spirit
Givings and takings
And all precious things.

Blesséd above all others
Are they
Who find themselves
When all else is gone
Still indestructible
Imperishable
Forever there.

THE RIVER

Li-Po and I have drunk
    from the same river
        but I downstream from him.

Our sandals of great longing
    have left wet prints
        along the willowed shore.

We watch the word-flower petals
    falling   floating   flowing
        on the darkness.

MANSION OF MIRRORS

Down corridors of mirrored doors
Of legends, myths and metaphors
    My restless spirit goes—
    Why—God only knows—
Among the never-evermores.

In labyrinths of space and time,
In epic prose and lyric rime,
    With symbols I compare
    What is and is not there
In thoughts and images sublime.

Though mirrors of infinity
Surround me with divinity,
    Until the day I die
    My spirit still must try
The door locks of Eternity.

REMEMBERING A GREEK POETESS

The fragrant color softly stays
    While gentle hands caress;
Cool petals glow as fancy plays
    Perfumes of tenderness.

The precious seeds of summer sown
    In storms of willingness
Are lost on unreceptive stone
    In fields of emptiness.

The dry stalk withers in the heart
    While winter's frozen lips
Caress a flower that falls apart
    Beneath pale fingertips.

REMEMBERING GOETHE, DONNE AND HEMINGWAY

Two guardian spirits never cease
    To battle in my breast:
The daemon of eternal peace,
    The demon of unrest.

I am all men of earthlings born,
    Forever torn apart,
Forever made to bear the thorn
    Of conflict in my heart.

It seems to me it is for this,
    For this the bell must toll:
On earth there is no lasting bliss,
    No quietude of soul.

SHAKESPEARE

One man of those whose written works I've known
    Was best able to make all things hold still
Beneath his pen. For me he stands alone
    In scope of thought, in feeling, and in skill.
I sometimes think he wrote not what he knew
    But what already lay upon the page
And he but traced it out, as children do
    Who draw their letters at an early age.

Day after day, with quill pen sharpened fine,
    He handspiked passion, held ambition fast;
Night after night, spun ink webs line on line
    Ensnaring all that moved, until at last,
In words immortal, his Genius had enshrined
The frailty and strength of humankind.

MICHELANGELO

Blow touching blow, I wonder, do you know
    Whose mallet throbs in heart and flesh and bone,
    Whose hands are these that strike upon the stone,
    That they are those of Michelangelo?
Hour by hour and day by day my slow
    Sharp chisel works while heavy timbers groan
    Beneath your weight, yet you are not alone,
    My David. Where you go I, too, must go.
Both you and I would more than earthly be;
    So pray us now, each for the other's sake
    To find our nobler selves with each blow struck,
For we shall live through all eternity
    If we fail not, be flawed, or straining break;
    Should God permit my hands to have good luck.

DAVID

Blow touching blow, I know, I know
The hands of Michelangelo!

Here within this roughhewn stone
His mallet throbs in flesh and bone.

Hour by hour and day by day
His chisel carves the Dark away.

His artist's heart aspires to see
His nobler self revealed in me.

While I, who wait within the stone
No longer face the Night alone.

We both would more than earthly be
To live through all eternity.

Each prays that for the other's sake
We shall not fail, be flawed, or break.

Now the last light stroke is struck,
Praise be to God, skilled hands and luck!

WILLIAM FAULKNER

Bottle in hand, face turned to the southern sky,
He watched the buzzards, sorted his life's
believings
And reckoned he, too, had feasted on carrion
leavings
Of the departed, and thought how a man must die
To provide for the future, and how all folks lie
At the end of their days in boxes of black
bereavings
Shameless as truth, stark naked of all
deceivings,
And he drank to the buzzards, sighed, and watched
them fly.

Unhated, unwanted, they wrote on the blankest blue
The stories and poems of life's unlucky
wayfarers
Whom nobody loved or needed; so gently they flew,
Without bother or danger, like black friars
At their prayers
Before feasting on alms, their black wings
sailing through
The labyrinth of time on the endless journey
of nowheres.

SEARCHERS

We listen, look and read
    With mind and heart,
Imploring in our need
    Each craft, each art.

We seek in sound and form,
    In paint and stone,
Direction of the storm
    We face alone.

In body and in word
    We try to know
What is not seen or heard
    That hurts us so.

The labored brush and pen,
    The dance and drum,
The chisel, guide us when,
    Unselved, we come.

With them we seek beyond
    Spent storm and stress
An all-resolving bond—
    Expressionless.

ARCHITECTURE

Designers are not builders
    As those of centuries past;
Neither plans nor buildings
    Are made to last.

The learning from the fingers
    That framed the towers of old
Is now machined and papered,
    Bloodless and cold.

But still the strains and tensions
    From winds that shriek and moan
Are everlasting agony
    In glass and stone.

Today the hearts of builders
    Who fear what they have built
Feel a deep uneasiness,
    A sense of guilt.

The dreams of masterbuilders,
    Of craftsmen long ago,
Are shards of windblown shattered glass
    On streets below.

HEART-FIRE

Promethean minds that bring the vital fire,
    Creating men from watery lumps of clay,
Are chained to what the least of men desire
    While eagles tear their inward dreams away.
No Herculean hand will set them free
    From worldly selfishness and human greed;
Pandora's evils swarm incessantly
    To sting and feed upon the flesh of need.
Beset with evils, chained forevermore,
    Promethean minds still labor at all things
To light immortal fires that will endure
    Beyond the eagles and Pandora's stings.
In all the world there is no nobler sight
Than heart-fire flaming through the dark of night.

NEW THINGS

New dreams are only the songs
    Forgotten until today,
Old songs with a new tune
    Sung in a different way.

New hopes are only the birds
    That fled before the snow,
Returning now in blossom time
    To places that they know.

New loves are only the waves
    Of a strange and distant sea,
Returning again from the boundless deep
    To touch the heart of me.

THE BLUES SINGER

Her voice held every word
In its arms
As if her heart would break
If left alone—
As if her soul would die
And life depart
With loving's last note sobbing
In her throat.

THE MEANING OF MEANING

"Nurture" is a soothing word
 And "nature", too, is gentle;
"Heredity" was harsh when heard
 As was "environmental".
Thus referential change occurred
 With change more fundamental.

When science changes what we know
 Some symbols are quite pliable
But others, spent, to history go
 With meaning unreliable.
Thus does our speech-work change and grow
 To reach the undeniable.

Essential truth is searching's goal
 But speaking the essential
To bring it gently to the soul
 Needs symbols reverential.
Thus literature and sacred scrolls
 Exalt the referential.

BRIGHT SWORD OF SONG

Plunge the bright sword of your song
    Into the ancient breast of Care
While there is time, and you are strong,
    And he is unaware.

And someday when you clasp a hilt
    From which the blade has dropped away,
You'll bless each glass of wine I've spilt
    To make you sing today.

THE BRIDGE OF WORDS

The bridge of words is hazardous at best—
    We tread on sounds, we feel the framework sway
Above time's deep abyss and when we rest
    The wind of silence drifts our thoughts away.

The names of things, the worn and weathered stones
    Of memoried piers sunk in the depths below,
Support our faith above the dark unknowns
    With awe and wonder from the long ago.

The bridgeworks of relations, too, have names
    In structured thought by which the mind and heart
Avert life's dangers and the soul maintains
    Its right of passage through the builder's art.

From shore to shore we fare, from birth to death,
    Upon a bridge of words from which we see
The visions that we breathe with sounding breath
    In song and prayer, in prose and poetry.

MEDITATION

I think I'll just drop in on God
When this day's work is done
Without a nick or note or nod
Or word to anyone.

I'll find Him in His studio
As He finds me in mine
When something goes as good things go
With craftsmanship divine.

We'll talk a bit and have a drink,
Discuss His work awhile;
Perhaps He'll ask me what I think,
Or look at me and smile

If I had trouble with the new
And never quite broke par;
If everything I tried to do
Was close—but no cigar.

Have one of mine, He may say then
And pass His box of leaves
Hand rolled in heaven for old men
By angels in shirt sleeves.

He has this way, an artist's way,
With ordinary folk
Of sharing more than He can say
As silently as smoke.

WILL THERE BE PRAYERS IN HEAVEN?

Will there be prayers in heaven
    And arts of space and time
Where everything is perfect
    In the Radiance sublime?

Will builders build cathedrals
    And sculptors speak with stone?
Will painters paint to glorify
    The spaceless One Alone?

Will there be songs and symphonies
    And dancing as before—
Will there be poems of longing
    In the timeless Evermore?

In heaven's spaceless timelessness
    What will become of Art
So chained to all creation—
    So earthbound in the heart?

BEAUTY

Thieves have told me of her: flashing bits
Of how they saw her in the things they stole.
And beggars say she gives with lavish grace,
But what she gives is neither bread nor meat
And one could starve in her munificence.
A common gossip monger, I have walked
With vendors of all things beneath the sun,
And with the ones who bought not knowing why;
And these, I think, have seen her least of all.
Poets have given her gowns of sheerest dreams
And cloaked her in the velvet of their phrase
But all their weaving and their patterned rags
Are only made to fit their thoughts of her.
They have some picture in their hearts to go by
When they fashion things concerning her:
A lovely doll, she walks their pages through,
Dressed in the finery they have made with words.
Through certain rooms of houses where I pass,
In children's laughter, and on women's faces
Something of her presence seems to linger.
Forest darkness breathless in the trees
May be her shadow as she walks the stars—
A girl, trim-ankled, stealing home at night
On golden stones across a stream of blue.

TRIAD OF BEAUTY

The art works of the heart and soul possess
    The tenderness of love, but intellect
With all its elegance is comfortless;
    It seems to be content with cold respect.

Perhaps the art of mind that contemplates
    The architectural structures of creation
Lacks certitude that man evaluates
    More dearly than the doubts of ideation.

Perhaps, as time goes on, the fortitude
    Of love and faith, of wondrous revelation,
Will free cold science from its solitude
    And with compassion end its alienation.

The human spirit seeks the last full measure
    Heart and soul and mind combined express;
Triad of beauty, this, our earthly treasure,
    Might well be glory, near to blessedness.

A QUESTION OF TASTE

Should symbols of the heart
    By faith and love created
Be soiled by hate and art,
    Be spoiled and desecrated?

Pause and think a little
    Of crosses, flags and faces
And those who burn and piddle
    Such things in public places.

What if our strength in prayer,
    The land we love today
The tenderness we share
    Were burned or stained away?

Our symbols are the signs
    Of all we love and cherish,
Our constant soul designs
    For hopes that never perish.

THE PIRANHAS

The piranhas have eaten a poet.
Tonight
He lies on the bottom
Among his own bones
And the bones of friends,
Safe in the deep waters
Of myth and legend
Washed with mystery.
Watching above
The black silhouettes
Of his destroyers
Herding and feasting
Upon the heavens,
Teeth nibbling stars
Tails splashing away
Galaxies
Reducing the firmament
To froth
And excrement.

MY SHADOW

Sometimes it goes before me,
    Sometimes it follows after;
    It may be brief as laughter
Or long as memory.

Sometimes it crooked lies
    In devious ways and clever;
    But truth to tell, it never
Is quite my natural size.

Sometimes in measured scrawl
    In moments of elation,
    In the white light of creation,
It isn't there at all.

COMEDY

To transmute life to laughter
    Well may be
What merry men are after
    In comedy—

To change the whole perspective
    Of what we see
From subjective to objective
    Reality—

To change us from tragedians
    And make us free
May be the true comedian's
    Alchemy.

Prepared for the hereafter,
    Bliss may be
To dwell with divine laughter
    Eternally.

ABSTRACTIONISM

Page white
Ink, night
Held pen, breath
Life/Death
Perspective lost
Boundaries crossed
Unconscious leeched
Limits reached
Hand nimbleness
Is symbolless
Impressionless
Expressionless
Imageless
In nothingness
Subtracted
Abstracted
Page white
(.)Night

AFTERTHOUGHT

Too many times we've heard it said—
"It just does not make any sense!"
Of both the living and the dead
Too many times we've heard it said
Of something that somebody read
With furrowed brow and eyes intense.
Too many times we've heard it said!
It just does not make any sense!

ALL CREATION IS A POEM

All creation is a poem to me—
The making of my soul's tranquility,
The thought about, the felt, is everywhere
In rhythms that I know and feel and share
With all that moves in heavenly harmony.

With all that is I rest content to be—
Whatever I may think or feel or see
Love reconciled with reverence, awe and prayer—
All creation is a poem to me.

Though meaning may remain a mystery—
Though understanding hold no certainty,
Still shall I feel it is my heart's affair
To make a memory of the glory there
In symbols of my soul's serenity.
All creation is a poem to me.

NATURE

OBSERVING THINGS

Observing things, this much I've found—
That some things burrow in the ground;
  Some things swarm and build like bees,
While other things go 'round and 'round
  Like planets, stars and galaxies.

It's not quite clear to me just why
Some things are earthbound, others fly;
  Some poke along li1ke tortoises,
While others float twixt earth and sky
  Like lobsters, fish and porpoises.

I have been told, if memory serves,
That nothing is what one observes;
  All things are only what we sense,
While mind creates in cranial nerves,
  Like God from chaos, form and essence.

Observing things, I plod my way
More awestruck with each passing day;
  Some things occasion tears or smiles,
While others some strange threat convey,
  Like hornets, snakes and crocodiles.

AFTER IMAGES

The azure trails behind blue butterflies,
  Green hummingbird rubescent iridescence,
Leave glimmering blossoms blooming in the eyes
  With bursts of never ending evanescence.

Dashing goldfish flashing leave behind
  Broad paths of sunshine shimmering in the heart;
Darkened fireflies flicker through the mind
  Like lanterns in the night when searchers part.

The azure wings, the ruby blushing throats,
  The golden scales, the phosphorescent glows
Leave trails of chills like wild symphonic notes,
  Like inkdrops burned in memory's melting snows.

HOLLYWOOD COYOTES

Through purple sage at dusk I hear
 Coyotes on the nearby hills
Singing to fire engine sirens
 Songs of love and rabbit kills.

They and I live on the edge
 Of urban slum vulgarity,
And making songs to sirens is
 With us no twilight rarity.

It fills my heart with savage glee
 To join their outcast company,
First in low antiphony
 And then in hairy harmony.

Our songs caress the chaparral,
 The cactus and the night owl's wings,
The monkey flower, the mariposa,
 Yucca blooms, and all wild things.

ONLY THE LONELY

A girl coyote friend I've found
 Is delicate as thistledown—
A shadowy shape, she slips around
 In chaparral above the town.

She has a queer bobtail of white,
 Not one of brown that proudly plumes;
Her left hind ankle's not quite right—
 An injury suffered, one presumes.

Since we are friends, I bring her things—
 She comes near when I softly whistle;
Store-bought chicken backs and wings
 She sweetly grinds up, bones and gristle.

We both are different in some ways
 That others scorn and criticize—
They'll never know our strange love days,
 The tenderness in our wild eyes.

MY LIZARD FRIEND

My lizard friend
    Is small and brown;
He suns himself
    With eyelids down.

When there's something
    Good to eat
He feels my tapping
    In his feet.

He slips across
    The desert sand
And leaps upon
    My outstretched hand.

Looks up at me
    And takes the fly;
We squash together,
    He and I.

The fly was good,
    The fly is gone;
That's something we
    Must think upon.

And presently
    He leaps away,
Provided for
    Another day.

LIZARDNESS

I have shed my lizard skin—
That's the shape that I was in.
If you don't like it, that's too bad—
It was the only shape I had.

Those little feet, those empty eyes
Have walked and watched in paradise
With crawlers, bugs and honeybees
Delicious in the flowering trees.

Though my lizard self is gone,
My lizardness still lingers on.
With every springtime you may find
Another skin I've left behind.

If you don't, do not despair—
My paradise will still be there.
Just shed whatever skin you're in
And be with me where I have been.

BREAKFAST FOR FOUR

This morning after break of dawn
The young doe with her dappled fawn
Drank the garden fountain dry
And breakfasted, as you and I.

They nibbled at the path's buffet
Of ivy vine and green display
Of buds and pink hibiscus flowers
To their delight, as well as ours.

We watched until they wandered on
And soon the two of them were gone
From fountain, flowers and ivy bed—
So much like us, so much unsaid.

BLUE ARROW

From hillside tree
    To redwood chair
A perfumed sea
    Of springtime air.
    She up there
I here below
    Juliet she
I Romeo
    Two lovers we
Whose wishes go
    Between the tree
And patio.

I clad in gray
    She clad in blue
Old man and jay
    In love, we two.
    Our hearts are true
To what we see
    Her arrowed way
Is dear to me
    But peanut pay
Distresses me
    Who cannot say
Love should be free.

REFLECTION

The frightened bird misjudged
The window's mirrored sky and trees
For Nature's truth.

The ants bear broken wings
Beyond the mirror's curtained darkness
Far from shattered images of light.

So die we all against what we believe
While angels watch and wait
Beneath the grass.

THE GRAY SQUIRREL

His right eye lost to springtime love,
To vicious, needle-fingered love,
    He plops upon the window sill
From eucalyptus limbs above
    And bends us to his rodent will.

A big gray squirrel, who wanted love,
A dangerous, hateful, spiteful love,
    White bellied, every inch a male,
Expectant of our every move
    He sits erect with plumey tail.

His one black eye, intent with love—
Peanut, walnut, almond love—
    He reaches out his hands to hold
The treasure he is fondest of—
    A slice of avocado gold.

With one bright orb not lost to love,
Not lost to vicious, spiteful love,
    He glares at us as if to cry,
"Somewhere, up there, in heaven above,
    I lost my head, my heart, my eye!"

CAT SPACE

Beyond the small togetherness of sex
    There is a wild, delicious loneliness—
The tiger, cougar and the bobcat vex
    Us naked bipeds with their onlyness.

Alone, they stalk the meat of daily need
    In guiltless freedom from the soft caress—
Each tree and rock, each insect, flower and weed
    Is only what it is—no more, no less.

The dawn, the morning, afternoon and night
    Will bring no dire distractions of distress—
Until sex calls again, all will be right
    In brief, delicious, wildcat loneliness.

VARIATION ON AN OLD THEME

When sudden variation strikes
    The generational chain
Of gradual growth and look-alikes
    Acceptance suffers strain.

When characters are changed too fast
    Mutation seems unwise,
Disturbing the familiar past
    With aberrant surprise.

Quick change of form or qualities
    Sometimes breaks the heart
As Nature's whimsicalities
    Set lovely lives apart.

White hummingbirds are never known
    To mate or nest together—
The white winged bluejay flies alone,
    Predestined by a feather.

I AM ONE OF THESE

The infinite variety
The individuality
Of all the creatures that I see
Amazes me.

I marvel to observe the ways
Each living thing its hunger stays—
How each one meets the nights and days
Its life obeys.

In wonderment of kindred things
With fins and paws, with hooves and wings—
With all that slithers, creeps and clings
My heart sings.

For I am one of these who go
With sky above and earth below
Until my footsteps grow too slow—
This I know.

TO THE EVENING STAR

Clear star of distant heaven,
Lamp that shines upon the roadway
Of eternity, along what evening dusk
Ran the first small soul that bore the torch
And paused in breathless flight
To give you flame?

What mad, mad ecstasy
Of the souls that followed,
Dancing the fire-dance, blown wild
With the wind, until all the lamps
Of all the great constellations
Flickered and gleamed!

Out of the lighted universe
In silent and stately procession
Passed the army of souls bearing the tapers.
Gone is the night,
Extinguished the lamp of the roadway;
Ghostly, the echo of footsteps
Walking the earth.

WHERE TALLOW DRIPS

Candles flicker in the stillness of the night;
Against the vaulted dome dark stand the spars,
And here stand I—and feel within my breast
The Unseen Breath that blows among the stars.

BELOVÉD STAR

Shall we infer,
    Viewed from afar,
That what you were
    Is what you are?

Shall we infer
    That what you are
Is what you were,
    Belovéd star?

Belovéd star,
    Shall we infer
That what we are
    Is what we were?

Shall we infer,
    Viewed from afar,
We only were
    But never are?

ASTEROID OR VOLCANO

I wonder what catastrophe
    Upset the apple cart—
Earth's wild reptilian dynasty.
I wonder what catastrophe,
By impact or explosively,
    Inspired the small mammalian heart.
I wonder what catastrophe
    Upset the apple cart.

THE CRYSTAL MYSTERY

Among the vast galactic realms of space,
    Within our planet's near magnetic field
We move and have our being, find our place
    By unseen lines of force to which we yield.

Micro-magnets guide the salmon's run,
    The pigeon and the wild goose in their flight;
More powerful than the storms that cloud the sun
    Are tiny crystals of the magnetite.

Sense organs of these things of air and sea
    Bear this compass of the iron oxide
That guides them home, wherever they may be,
    Across the spinning vastness wild and wide.

Is it too much to seek within the soul
    The crystal mystery of the lodestone there
That we might reach some far magnetic pole—
    Some field of force of which we're unaware?

TOTAL ECLIPSE

As the moon blots out the circle of the sun
    Telescopic charioteers
    Race around the hemispheres
And the carousel is fun
    When the lovely diamond ring of light appears.

But as wheels of glass in harmony respond
    To the music of the spheres
    And the time of grasping nears
To engage the Great Beyond
    The lovely diamond ring just disappears.

When the sun again is shining blinding bright
    On earthly chanticleers
    The enchanted charioteers
Who raced the day's brief night
    Race on to reach the ring in lost light years.

THEORY AND DIVINITY

The attraction of all things to one another—
The gravitational fields we share—all hold
Our universe in space-time nets that fold
Our hearts to Heaven, our lives to our Earth-mother.

Our vast imaginings and dreams we verify—
As best we can—with eye and symboled story
In Reason's net of mode and category
Too frail for faith, too weak to satisfy.

With brief, provisional truths we improvise
Some furtherance of our knowledge as we grasp
At strands of Being—yet in these we clasp
A Power beyond our powers to theorize.

With strands of Being we are bound forever
In everlasting unity sublime—
Our oneness is a binding more divine
Than theory dreams, or death itself can sever.

SEA SHELLS

Bygone hours of spent emotion
    Swept by memory's tidal hand
Lie like shells cast from the ocean
    Bleached and empty on the sand.

The glistening shells are smiled upon
    By all who walk beside the sea
And touch the dwellings of the gone
    With reverential intimacy.

From memoried depths the past ascending,
    Swept by cloud and wind to land,
Paints a rainbowed arch transcending
    Empty sea shells on the sand.

FOOTPRINTS

At low tide when deep forces take
  The ocean from our reach
We who walk with sadness make
  Bright footprints on the beach.

But when the high tide seeks the land
  And rushes to the shore
White water foams across the sand
  And footprints are no more.

Time and tide our hearts deceive—
  The waves wash on and on—
The rivulets of tears they leave
  Glisten, then are gone.

DAWN FISHERMAN

The wet line flashes through the wave,
  The bright reel sings beneath the thumb;
A thread of joy runs through the grave;
  The fish are wise; the fish are dumb.

The bamboo bends against a cloud,
  The shadow curves upon the sand;
Gray silver spray is like a shroud,
  The barb is better than the hand.

Some trust to luck, some have a rule,
  But when the reel at last is wound,
The thread drips cold upon the spool
  And Death weighs scarcely half a pound.

EVENING FISHING

The wet petals
Of daisies
Brushing my knees.

Locust flowers
Hanging in clusters
Touching my cheek.

The sigh of the boat
The dip of oars
A gentle swish
Listening.

Far away fish
Breaking the water.

A dry fly
Offered
Light as a heartbeat
Upon the stillness.

TIME

My moments are the petals
    Of the flowers;
The sundials of the forest
    Tell my hours.

My days and months are told
    With golden spheres;
The fossiled stones on mountains
    Tell my years.

My flowers and forest trees,
    My stars and rocks
Tell all I need of time
    That laughs at clocks.

TO A BLACK MAN

John Butler, hitch the wagon up
    And give the lines a swing;
Let's make off to the thickets
    In back of Bentley's spring.

Down the road, John Butler,
    The way we used to go—
My short brown legs a'swingin'
    From the high seat to and fro.

For it's early morn, John Butler,
    And the dew is on the grass,
And we go to cut the bean poles
    From the fragrant sassafras.

Down the road a'joggin'
    With the lines a'hangin' free
And the singletree a'clinkin',
    It all comes back to me

For it's spring again, John Butler,
    And the dew is on the grass,
And it's time to cut the bean poles
    From the fragrant sassafras.

OCTOBER'S COME AT LAST

Through the leaves, through the leaves
    Wandering through the past—
Golden leaves to tell my heart
    October's come at last.

Through the leaves, through the trees,
    Hidden lies the way.
I wonder, were the leaves so deep
    A year ago today?

Wandering lost among the trees
    This alone I know—
October, too, will soon be gone
    And bright gold turned to snow.

AUGUST

Morning comes like a mean dog
Over the hills,
Baring his teeth
Dripping his red tongue.

These are the days
When dogs go mad,
And green scum
Covers the duck pond.

Curled leaves clatter
Through dry trees,
And far away
Is the sound of knives
Chopping
In the cornfields.

INDIAN SUMMER

I wonder, will this vast Creation know
   The sweet, sad time of autumn and of men
Between the first frost and the winter's snow
   That makes a smoky wonderland, and then
   Renews the joy of chisel, brush and pen?

I wonder, will Creation find a way
   Between the first foreboding chill of death
And winter's final ice to gently lay
   Before death's door, with its remaining breath,
The reborn promise of a springtime day?

I wonder, will there be a glorious haze
   When summer's gone and warning first frosts cease?
   I wonder, will Creation's Hand release
The beauty, truth and love of springtime days
   In autumn's sweet serenity and peace?

KINDRED OF THE TREE

When tall trees yellow for the rain
  And curl their parched leaves up,
Beneath the earth dark fingers strain
  To reach a buried cup.

Dry branches clasp a cloudless sky;
  Twisted with a cruel lust,
The sheets of bark scale off and lie
  As old gloves in the dust.

Some men are kindred of the tree.
  They thirst, and know the pain
Of things which never shall be free
  Until they feel the rain.

Such men have hands that sometimes sift
  A little soil that's dry.
They watch the winds, or stand and lift
  Their faces to the sky.

NEIGHBORHOOD CHORE

My neighbor's gone a'traveling
  And left his yard behind
With all the fallen twigs and leaves
  That come down with the wind.

Today I raked my neighbor's yard
  And felt a pleasant thrill,
As if I'd clipped his coupon bonds
  Or dipped into his till.

The piles of rustling, golden loot
  Are mine and mine alone;
While he's a stranger, God knows where,
  I've fleeced him to the bone.

I've wealth to burn, and burn I will,
  But it will be most hard,
When he comes home, to take his thanks
  And give him back his yard.

WINTER DAWN

I stand beside my window stiff with cold
    To meet the winter morning's feeble light,
To reach for sunrise, and release my hold
    Upon the perilous edge of remanant night.
The drift of wind and leaf and moon and snow
    Disturb the fading darkness, then is gone;
The gray-banked clouds pile high their icy floe
    To block the narrow channel of the dawn.

I am the captain of a frozen ship
    That stiffened as she sailed to glittering glass.
Through crystal lines bright splinters leap and slip;
    Through shattered mirrors flickering heartbeats pass.
My brittle bones are marrow-iced, and few
Have ever been so wintered through and through.

SNOW

The snowflakes fall upon the evergreen
    In silent grandeur when the woods are still,
    Slowly, gently, hour by hour until
The verdant boughs beneath their silver sheen
Bend down to earth. How gracefully they lean,
These things of nature, toward the great unseen
    Beautifully bowed, nor fear the darkening chill
    That sweeps the glade and blows from hill to hill
While I, in deepest mystery, walk between.

Beneath my feet there sleeps a summer night
    Of katydids and tree frogs great with song
Where fireflies signal intermittent light
    And through the dark the unhoused snail walks along.
In daisied fields beneath this world of white
    I hear warm crickets caroling loud and strong.

WOODS IN WINTER

Let me walk softly on the winter snow
And deep into the woods as wild things go,
    As if it were my home, to find my youthful vows
Summer buried, waiting in the glow
    Of sunset shadowed through the barren boughs.

Let me exhume my treasure late remembered,
Redolent of earth and cold Decembered,
    To feed my hunger for the flowering spring
Before my hopes were slaughtered and dismembered,
    While still the sun lay warm on leaf and wing.

Let me be gentle with my vows forsaken
And all the ways through life that were mistaken,
    For this was meant to be, as now I know
If new songs in my wintered heart awaken
    I'll walk as one twice blessed on flowering snow.

LAUGHTER IN THE TREES

Chill laughter in the trees brings down the gold
With blackened fingers reaching heaven high.
These fingers make a web, now ages old,
To seine the starlight from the winter sky.

Inside my heart the icy laughter splinters
Things that died because there was no sun.
The permeating gloom of many winters
Made them frail and killed them one by one.

And now these fingers, reaching through the sky,
Would take the starlight too, and hide the gold.
The snow is yet too dry for tears, and I
Have none to shed upon a world so cold.

HELLEBORES

When I have done the winter's chores
    Oh, wouldn't it be nice
To skate on flowering hellebores
    That bloom beneath the ice!

In sunshine on a winter's day
    Upon a flowering pond,
On silver skates I'd skim along
    To glory and beyond.

For I believe in hellebores
    Sun-laced in lilac ice,
Cream-pink and real as winter's chores,
    As real as paradise.

BEYOND THE WEATHER

Sometimes the mightiest trees are slain
    Before the tempest passes,
While fingers of the wind and rain
    Caress the moss and grasses.

But when a drouth is everywhere
    And sunshine is the weather—
When soil and sand are parched and bare
    All things are slain together.

Be moss and grass when wild winds drive
    The storm clouds in their flying—
Be seed that sleeps and will survive
    Beyond the dead and dying.

THE LAST MOUNTAIN

While the timber wolves howl
And the devil winds blow,
I must climb the last mountain
Through darkness and snow.

I must climb to the black pines
That cry in the night
On the breast of the mountain
Storm shrouded in white.

I must climb to the wild rain
Of hailstones that beat
On the scrub and the split-rock
Deep buried in sleet.

I must climb to the storm clouds
That weep as they hold
To the stones of the mountain top
Barren and cold.

I must reach the wild fury
Where bright crystals form
In the depths of the tempest,
In the heart of the storm.

I must climb the last mountain
Through darkness and snow,
While the timber wolves howl
And the devil winds blow.

THE RIVER GOD

Today I saw the River God beneath a willow tree
Grubbing at the roots with a red, watery hand.
Gently he unlaced them to the rain swollen current
Gently, so gently, that he didn't break one.

THE OLEANDERS

The wind
Took white petals of oleander
Falling upon a blue lake
In starlight
Drove them shoreward
With a sudden breath
Shattered
A thousand sails
Against the earth.

The night
That heard our footsteps pass
Like laughter
Through the oleander trees
Drew us earthward
We knew not how
Destroyed
A thousand dreams
We knew not why.

FROM A JAPANESE PRINT

I thought of a blue, cold mountain
        Where a lone pine
Painted the silver margin of the moon
        With brush strokes
        Of the night wind.

THE WEB

On morning wind
The web
Arachne loomed
Pursuing death
Alone last night
Entangles
One more mortal face.

THE LOST PEARL

The dying oyster
Unshells its pain
Upon the breast
Of acid death
In cold
Light lustrous tears.

LOST INNOCENCE

In a far place
Snowflakes
Ravished by spring rain
Disappeared
Sobbing upon the breast
Of long ago.

THREE RAINDROPS

One fell on a pale hand
That stroked a lady's hair

Another on a green leaf
To set a diamond there

The last fell on the lily pond
And vanished everywhere.

STARLIGHT

The blue nest
Of night
Is a wind of stillness
Where gold wings
Rest
In flight.

METEOR SHOWER

Firefalls
Of embers
Heaven's
Furnace
Shaking glory
Down
To ashes.

LOST

Green sunlit water
Showers of goldfish
The lily pads among.

In your eyes
The golden glint
Of barbed selection
For the beautiful
The strong
The perfect one
When we were young.

A wish
A step
A word
And all were gone
Lost
The lily pads among
When we were young.

MORNING SADNESS

Cherry blossoms
Iced
With frozen rain
Are weeping
Iridescent
Tears.

FRAGMENTS

Their meaning fled
Only the dead skins
Of all the words love penned
Remain.

They cling—
Dry locust husks upon the bark
Of maples
In the spring—
Dry lizard tissue caught
Between the cracks
Of rocks that peeled
The hurt away.

They cling to paper
As the dried flies cling
To spider web
The spider gone
Devoured by spinning wind
By beak of time.

FLOWERING PLUM

Plum blossoms caught like snowflakes
    On branches thin and spare
Are springtime's tiny heartaches
    When sunlight lingers there.

So dearest dear are things like these
    When dark clouds come again
And heartaches melt to memories
    In sorrow's summer rain.

GARDEN MORNING

The birdbath overflows—
Wet wings shower mirrored blossoms
With rainbows of song.

Turquoise lizard arms
Embrace the eucalyptus tree
Fragrant in the sun.

Night bandit fingerprints
Where masked raccoon stole goldfish
Dry along the path.

Frail ivy holds the stones
Of granite walls as shadows
Melt the golden hills.

SEASONS CHANGE

It used to be that apples red
    Upon a summer bough
Would fill me with a hot desire
    To pluck and taste, but now
I like to come and stand beneath
    An apple tree that's bare
And feel November's icy hand
    Upon my grizzled hair.

IN MY GARDEN

It takes a gloomy day to bring you back—
Damp shadows clinging to a wall,
Wet leaves upon the roofs, and sodden walks.

Rain-wet pears let go the branch and fall
Thump on the ground. I let them lie.

At nine o'clock the hollyhocks are lovely;
By ten the garden bench will be quite dry.

THE BREAKWATER

The sea put down her arms
On the rocks of the breakwater
And sobbed
As her hair surged shoreward
In long tumbles of foam
And she cried
In deep slow swells of remembrance
While small craft
Safe in the harbor
Rocked gently
In a wash of tears.

VIGIL

I, who love the wind's sweet kiss
    And care not when she blows,
Must wisely dare not speak of bliss
    Nor dream of heart's repose.

I, who love the long-stemmed flower—
    Pond lily, garden rose—
Know not which one within the hour
    Shall bloom; nobody knows.

Keep free, my heart, to meet the kiss,
    To greet the fair, unfolding flower;
Be watchful, lest in sleep we miss
    The wind, the hour.

FLOOD

Rain was like blood on the cables of empty bridges,
    And wind was a dirge above rivers heavy with clay.
Men stood in their wet boots on the high ridges;
    Saw cattle and tools, saw everything carried away.
"We've saved ourselves," one said, "but the land is gone."
    "My house was new," said another, and picked up a stone
And threw it. "By god, you'd think...." his lips were drawn
    Tight as a sewed sack, and he walked off alone.

"You men ought to dry out your clothes." The tone was sharp.
    A man offered matches. "I guess they got wet," he said.
A boy's cold thumb struck twice on a Jew's harp
    Pressed to his teeth. A man in the group turned his head.
"It's all right, son—if you want to, go on and play."
But the boy stood still, and he put the harp away.

THIRST

All who dwell in deserts know
    The dread of everlasting drying—
They shudder when the sandstorms blow
    And all that lives is slowly dying.

Elliptically, by Heaven swirled
    In time's eternal loop of being,
The sand dunes move as moves the world—
    Too slowly for the eyes of seeing.

From fire to ice and back again,
    Along its going and returning
The desert lives or dies with rain
    In its blooming and its burning.

In wastelands of the heart and mind
    All with Heaven's Will are striving—
We thirst, we die, to leave behind
    Our blossoms, ashes, us surviving.

A HUNDRED YEARS

A hundred years!
Who cares for a hundred years?
    They counted the cash, they laughed,
    They called it cheap.
While rain on those evil days
Was meeker than tears,
    And wind was calm as a shepherd
    Counting his sheep.
A hundred years, and the soil
Flowed down from the ridges;
    A hundred years, and the prairies
    Were swirled away.
The richness of earth bled oceanward
Under the bridges,
    In the wake of the plow men cursed
    The rocks and the clay.

They fed in the furrows like sparrows
Without thought or care,
    They cut down the trees with the fury
    Of wind driven fire;
They sharpened the ax and the saw,
They broadened the share,
    They counted the cash through a hundred
    Years of desire.
While rain that was meeker than tears
    Held the knife to earth's side
And wind that was calm as a shepherd
    Sang while she died.

THE WINDS OF CHANGE

Across the barriers of the land and sea
    The winds of change blow men like wildflower seed
    In never ending gales of need and greed
To fall where chance and destiny decree.
While still upon the wind their liberty
    Is sweet with sunlight, without care or heed
    Until the fateful calm has done its deed

And they have fallen, now no longer free.
Imprisoned then on alien soil, they wait
To be transformed when dormancy is gone—
To bear the perilous last uncertainty
Of vital fire—to die or germinate—
To flower again and cast fresh seed upon
The winds of change, the calm of destiny.

THE DESERT

We had so much but still we wanted more—
We were like nomads parched with inward fire,
Forever thirsting as we wandered o'er
The never ending desert of desire.
The green oases in the burning sun
Glimmered and were gone; the wind-whipped sands
Built scorching dunes where crystal streams had run
And lakes dried up beneath our outstretched hands.
Our tracks across the wasteland led to nowhere—
The heatwaves of our passion failed to last;
Where once bright flowers and gardens filled the air
The desert now is empty, dark and vast.
Our avarice seemed so right just yesterday—
We were so sure—before we lost our way.

THE GREENHOUSE EFFECT

Will there be fire from heaven
In the greenhouse of tomorrow
Beneath the fragile canopy
That shades the planet's sorrow?

Will there be fire and ashes
On winds of retribution
That sweep the planet clean of guilt
In cosmic absolution?

Will science now be prophecy
Fulfilled in woe and sorrow?
On earth's revolving spit we turn,
Fearful of tomorrow.

TO FREEDOM

The mountain meadow grasses wave
The eagle on its wind blown way;
Each moment brings the shadowy wings
A heartbeat closer to the prey
The grasses have no power to save.

The sunlight falls upon the brave
Death struggle in the verdant vale;
The mountains cry against the sky,
The grasses bleed to no avail,
Talon torn, on Freedom's grave.

RAIN

He said to me, "When rain falls on my roof
And wets the fields I've planted with such care—
When it gathers in the prints of paw and hoof—
I think it must be falling everywhere.

This is my world, and people laugh at me
When I express in words how much it means
To see the raindrops shine on grass and tree
And give new life to fields of corn and beans.

They say my world is much too small and I
Should think and feel beyond my barns and fences—
They miss the point that what falls from the sky
Is not put down as income and expenses.

There's no use saying all things suffer pain
When they're deprived of what they need to live—
That when I stand and watch the falling rain
I would to God I had as much to give."

FOOD CHAIN

Struggle
Is ridiculous
As well as vain
If you're far down
Or near, or at
The bottom
Of the food chain.

Quickly eaten things
Do not complain—
You have to be far up
Or near, or at
The top to feel
The full futility
Of pain.

Struggle
Is ridiculous
As well as vain—
Morsel that you are
You're edible
And so am I—
Again, again and again.

AFTER THE STORM

The eucalyptus limbs are bare
    As pink-and-water-satin skin;
Wet bark and leaves lie everywhere,
    And soon the clean-up must begin.

The storm is over now, but I
    Am in the treetops, blowing still;
While shreds of torn clouds race the sky
    I kiss and cling against my will.

The water-satin limbs that shine
    Rain-silvered, storm released at last,
Are mine again, still safely mine,
    Now the violent hour is past.

CHANGE

Once again the vast uncertainty
    Of nature calms the dread
Uncertainty of life. Rock and star
And chromosome were never what they are
    And nothing dead is absolutely dead.

For there is change. The vast uncertainty
    Of change excites the dust
Bewilderingly. The endless wax and wane
Of space and time are Nature's hurricane:
    We ride the storm of change; in chance we trust.

Once again the vast uncertainty
    Of Nature calms the mind
But brings great weariness. Impermanence
Becomes, at last, a sorry recompense,
    And what we seek is lost in what we find.

NATURE IS A WONDER

Nature hates a saver
    As sure as dirt and dust!
And that's not just palaver—
    It's true as rot and rust.

She plagues the treasure trover
    With every worm and bug—
If anything's left over
    It's swept beneath the rug.

The sawdust and the screaming
    Of prayer books made from trees;
The suffering and the dreaming,
    The songs and memories—

Like lint and fuzz, go under
    The rug, the chair, the cot—
Ah, Nature is a wonder
    But tidy she is not.

OPUNTIA

Old water bags, old water bags,
    My cactus friend, this hour
Around your feet are tattered rags
    And in your hat a flower.

I touch your spines, which undermines
    Our friendship, yet I know
You must protect the soft confines
    Where precious waters flow.

We stand as one in summer sun,
    Old cactus friend, and share
The spiny hurt that must be done
    When we're touched anywhere.

THE GOLDENROD

When I was young I strolled among
    Wild fields of goldenrod;
I breathed the wind, I drank the sun—
    I never thought of God.

Now I am old, the fields of gold
    Are withered, yet one rod
Of faded gold I lift and hold
    Awhile for love of God.

In wintry wind, with clouded sun—
    With silent stone and clod—
No longer young, I wait among
    The fallow fields of God.

SPRINGTIME CHINESE WISTERIA

Upon the lattice laced
    Bare woody vines
Bone dry and winter placed
    Make shadowed lines
Against the redwood siding.
    Still, in the deep
Arterial depths abiding
    Love wakes from sleep.

Unfolding racemes grow
    Pale blossomed, turning,
Eyes closed and all aglow
    With sunshine yearning.
Then comes the purple hour
    Of full awakening,
Full passioned, full in flower,
    Heartaching.

Upon the lattice still
    No leaf is seen;
Below the window sill
    No blade of green.
Yet, in this purple bed
    Sleep verdant vines,
Dry pods when passion's fled
    And time's dark lines.

AMARYLLIS

Theocritis and Virgil said your name
As now I say it softly in my garden;
Edmund Spenser, too, breathed you to fame—
Of all such lofty souls, I beg their pardon.

For you to me are just a fragrant girl
Fresh from her bath, a rose-pink naked lady;
Slim of limb, you set my thoughts awhirl
In August heat, beneath trees cool and shady.

Of all my garden flowers, you come to me
Warm and fragrant with love's naked hunger,
And I recall how sweet it used to be
With someone that I knew when I was younger.

MONKEY FLOWERS

The toasted hills are buttered bright
With dabs of monkey flowers
Capering in the shimmering light
Of circus summer hours.

Comedians of the buttery face,
Laughing flowers of fun,
On slippery slides they ride and race,
Tumbling in the sun.

Sticky monkey mimics all,
Grimacing, falling down,
With gimmick horns and bells they call,
"Come up and be a clown!"

CUPS OF GOLD

Perfumed strumpets
Blowing yellow
Golden trumpets
Down the alleys
Of the night—

Yellow golden
Nocturne fragrance
Spilled from valleys
Of delight—

Dreamy trumpets
Naughty strumpets
Alleys
Valleys
Fragrance
Vagrance
In the trellised
Warm moonlight.

HIBISCUS FLOWERS

Furled umbrella flowers
Of pink hibiscus
Enwrap the joy of life and death
In secret scrolls.

Upturned against the darkness
Of the earth,
The heavenly rain, the sun, the stars
Are folded home.

In winding sheets of faded pink
The stamens and the pistils
Sleep the sleep
Of beauty done.

Oh, might we all
Be shrouded so, our spirits spent,
In faded beauty's petaled arms
Hibiscus like.

WHITE ORCHID TREE

When I first saw
    The orchid tree
Its boughs were snowed
    With chastity.

Soon every blossom
    Was a pod
Bursting in
    The hand of God.

On careless winds
    Unbridled blown
To bird and rock
    The seeds were thrown.

And yet to me
    One seed fell true
To flower again
    As I in you.

TREE TRIMMING TIME

Today they're trimming all the trees—
    Green foliage, sighing, gently falls,
Drifted by the springtime breeze
    On granite ivy-covered walls.

Birds and squirrels seek safety now
    To watch the storm of saw and blade,
Their falling world in every bough,
    Disaster in the homes they made.

Only wise men in the tree tops
    Know what they do is for the best,
That new boughs grow when trimming stops
    Above the fallen, shattered nests.

On lovely limbs the squirrels will play,
    The shattered nests will be rebuilt;
The birds will sing again one day
    Where now are firewood, trash and guilt.

ENTICEMENT

Weave me a wreath of dogwood and violets
Gathered in a patch of sunshine.
                                        A blue bird's feather
Shall be your pay, and I will tell you
Where the wild grapes grow, and make a swing for you
Out of old vines hanging from the trees.
I will show you where the brown thrush
Builds her nest, and how a raccoon's track
Is like a tiny hand pressed in the mud.
Under an old log there is a great spider
Will teach us to make gossamer nets
To catch dew-pearls in the moonlight.
                                        There will be
Willow whistles when the sap is flowing,
And tea parties with toast-brown acorns
For cups and saucers. At night we shall sleep
On a bed of maple leaves that smell of the sun.
                                        Why do you wait,
Gathering your bundle of frail, dry twigs?
Is it for blackbirds going south, or wild geese
In the evening sky? Come, see how the slender birch
Weaves her shadow in the green water
Of my aloneness.

HOME, WHERE THE TREES WERE

Home was where the trees were:
    I remember
Scarlet and silver maples
And the samara-laden April wind;
Locusts, loud with bees,
Box elders,
Mockers, and the moon on ivory
    saucers
In tulip trees.

Home was where the trees were:
    I remember
Pitch pine and the pencil cedar

Resinous in hot September;
Mountain oak, warm rain,
Black walnut,
Afternoon, and the soundless purple
    earth
In mulberry lane.

Dream-torn, drenched with the
    white lilac,
Before sleeping
The thorn grows red
On the green briar creeping.
And the heart, like a swollen
    chestnut bur,
Snaps in the dark, remembering
Home, where the trees were.

COMPANION OCTAVES

Today I put my face against the sky
    And breathed more deeply than a mortal should:
    A breath so rich, so clean, so heaven-good
That to exhale it seemed almost to die.
An hour, a day, a year might have gone by
    While to that breath I clung, while there I stood—
    A figure tense, hewed from a living wood—
And breathed the entire distance of the sky.

With Phoebus westward driving through the blue,
    Past Hermes' gentle herd that cropped sweet air,
    My spirit flew, and all the world was fair.
No happy god, if ancient myths are true,
Felt more of life, lived more in moments few
    Than I lived then, when heaven touched my face,
    And listening earth, all with a woman's grace,
Looked up and smiled, and smiling so, withdrew.

WAITING

The green water of the long cascade
Leaps downward.

I have scraped the moss from the rocks
With wet hands
And killed a leaf
A thousand raindrops
Could not crush.

When starlight falls in a long cascade
All through the night
Upon my heart
I am like green moss

Waiting...

SURVIVAL

Roost with the owl
Upon the tree,
Fly with the hawk,
Keep fed, keep free.
Be mouse and snake,
Be squirrel and hare;
Day and night
Be quick, beware
And pray to God
To guide your flight,
To hear your squawk
On bough and sod,
To bless you as you
Squeak and howl,
And for His sake
Share blood and breath;
With Him partake
Of life and death.

PERSPECTIVES

THE WONDER OF THINGS

I am overcome with the wonder of things:
This hand,
    This ink, this pen,
    These letters upon the page,
These fingers, these scarred nails,
This little stand,
    This briar, darkened
    With nicotined tar and age,
And the smoke curling, this match
Discarded now,
    Its beautiful flame passed on,
    This book-lined room
Filled with the thoughts
Of wiser men, somehow
    Made mine by reading.
    Dust, even the gloom
Of the corners is wonderful:
Arachnid cathedrals rise
    In the destined trihedrons
    Of space where strange rites
Are performed, geometry practiced,
And dessicated flies,
    Swing on the measured ropes
    Through the long nights.
There should be candles, Bach,
And incensed air
    For the wonder of things
    And the dry flies hanging there.

PREMONITION

There is a madness in the world today—
    A kind of frenzy moving us to do
    Strange protective deeds, as if we knew
Of some impending doom, yet cannot say
That it is knowledge in the usual way
    Of thinking what is false and what is true,
    But more a felt awareness flowing through
All things about to break as they decay.

There is a quiver in the atmosphere,
    A seismic tremor in the earthly clay,
A whisper in the wind no ear can hear,
    A faltering of the stars that go astray—
There is the urge to clutch the near and dear
    Against we know not what, let come what may.

PROBLEM CHILD

Energy, water and toxic waste,
    Schools where few can learn,
Morality, war, and abominable taste
    Are matters of deep concern.

Uncivilized man is the problem child
    Of Nature wed to Time,
Bright of mind, but still half wild,
    Half monster, half sublime.

Solutions that he cannot see,
    Thoughts still not in his head
Await the day when he will be
    More civilized—or dead.

PURE SCIENCE

They bent their backs, broke rock, to build a road
    Where other men should walk and see the stars:
Geometrized weak arms to lift the load;
    They stormed the prisoned mind, they broke the bars.
With arcane symbols they discovered facts,
    Equationed mystery, and put wings to thought,
But withheld judgment as to moral acts:
    What man can do, he does—not what he ought.

They brought the brilliant light by which we see
    The world that lies beneath the world of sight,
The world beyond our vision, yet to be
    In time to come, with truth so dazzling bright,
How tragic, lost in darkness, now to find
The light by which we see has left us blind.

ENLIGHTENMENT

The mind outruns the body of mankind:
    Philosophy and science race ahead
    Along the paths of their illustrious dead
Who, too, left helpless multitudes behind.
The symboled universe by thought designed
    Lays like an arcane manuscript outspread,
    By all, save scholars, doomed to go unread;
To all, save thinkers, useless to the mind.

Technology and change accelerate
    The distance of the many from the few;
The Age of Information will not wait;
    The old beliefs persist beside the new;
Assimilation, slow at best, comes late;
    Enlightenment engulfs both false and true.

IMMENSITIES

Our numbered world grows much too vast for me,
    A myriad names for things confuse my mind;
Immensities of thought have come to be
    A burden and a babble to mankind.

Immensities have made my life shrink small,
    My earthly ties grow meaningless and weak;
I'm really almost nothing after all—
    Too trivial to count, too poor to speak.

Yet what I feel embraces all creation;
    While names and numbers fill me with despair,
Deep in my heart there is no alienation—
    My silent love and faith are always there.

Immensities have stilled my voice, and yet
    The need to tell my joy grows day by day,
As if Creation's Self would not forget
    If I but willed the glow I cannot say.

LARGE NUMBERS

The human mind has found peculiar tricks—
    Some good, some bad, and some outright deceptive—
    To handle numbers larger than receptive
Little brains can cope with and affix
Their meaning to the weak arithmetics
    Of home and marketplace where things perceptive
    Fit the fingers and the large conceptive
Things are left to science and to politics.

A thousand million make a billion, so
    Just drop some zeros for the presentation
        Saving space for sake of comprehension.
A thousand billion is a trillion, go
    From thence to sub and super numeration
        And there rest safe, beyond all apprehension!

THE MADNESS OF DESIRE

The madness of unsatisfied desires
    Afflicts the many as it does the few.
Insatiable, the lust for more conspires
    With power to challenge, conquer and subdue.
Frustration of desire leads all to deeds
    Bizarre and devious, foolish and inane;
The object sought grows grander as it feeds
    Upon the fevered heart that lusts in vain.
Unrequited love, ambition thwarted,
    Adventures brought to nought, inaptitude,
Make mad the dream-devoured and burning-hearted
    Dispossessed of rational rectitude.
Unsatisfied desires are red-hot coals
That madmen walk, asylumed in their souls.

LISTS

Sometime, somewhere, in some safe cave perhaps,
    The first man made a list with stick and sand
Of births and deaths and suns and life's mishaps
    Beyond his power to change or understand.
He made his marks for things to do tomorrow:
    To kill, to eat, to sleep, perhaps to go
Beyond the bleached bones of remembered sorrow—
    A man against the wind of long ago.
Since then his list has been man's history,
    Man's ordered catalogue of all things past
And all things yet to come; its mystery
    Pervades all temporal deeds from first to last.
Man lists his hopes, his dreams, his memories,
And listing, lives by his priorities.

MEANDERINGS

I feel my world meandering in its course—
    A stream that Nature's forces cause to bend.
Somewhere was there a reason and a source?
    Somewhere is there a purpose and an end?

From all who seek beginnings earth conceals
    The past in shrouds of darkness evermore;
To all who seek the end no search reveals
    What lies beyond bright heaven's farthest door.

Mid-stream I stand and let my thoughts flow by,
    Meandering with the forces deep below,
Content to drift until the stream runs dry—
    Resigned to all that I shall never know.

THE PUZZLE

The puzzle of equality
Is one of plain priority
As order is made manifest
In Nature's grim unrest.

The problem is of quality,
Position, rank and urgency,
Of privilege, power and precedent,
Of merit, need and accident.

The puzzle is to legalize
The fiction we idealize
While pressures of priority
Contradict equality.

The answer is to countervail
Conflicts Nature's laws entail—
To seek beyond what may not be
The Order of Eternity.

ENTROPY

All things seem to self-destruct—
    Repairing them's a bother;
Clocks run down and things deduct
    What's left from one another.

The universe to all intents
    And purposes is rubble
Nothing that the mind invents
    Can quite clear up the trouble.

The system seems as if devised
    To plague and irritate—
Disorganize the organized
    And then disintegrate.

But that is what it's all about:
    Celestial agitation;
This must be it, without a doubt—
    The chaos of creation.

COMPLEXITY

Of all our needs, the need to simplify
    Complex existence, nature's wild creation,
Has been the need most hard to satisfy—
    The most resistant to our ideation.
Our paths of thought are marked with vain endeavor
    To vanquish ignorance as a mortal curse—
To unify and simplify forever
    The way our minds perceive the universe.
Our world of morals, bequeathed us by tradition,
    Our world of reason, taken as a whole,
Are both too complex for the frail condition
    In which we seek to satisfy the soul.
Our knowledge yields no firm felicity—
Uncertain darkness shields simplicity.

WE ARE THE UNION

We are the thousand-and-one distinguishable fragments
    Bolted, riveted, spiked, welded and pressed;
Bent, forced, sprung, joined into segments,
    Lifted, fitted, assembled and ready for test.
We are the unified, structured, gigantic aggregate
    Of great construction, passing the world's inspection;
We move by strains and tensions that well might separate
    Chamber from weaker chamber, section from section.

We are the parts unequal of strength and duration,
    Bits of material, replaceable, ready to hand,
Molded and melted, built in the shape of a nation
    Fulfilling the mighty promise of a great land.
We are the Union, the powerful, the many-guided,
Moving by stresses and pressures, but undivided.

WE ARE THE BUILDERS OF SHIPS

We are the builders of ships, the dreamers in steel,
    Fairing the line and curve of invincible hulls.
Ours is the rake of the bow, the set of the keel,
    And the salt wind thrill of a thousand harbor gulls
Circling above the shipyard, above the ways
    Where the ships are building, and a thousand riveting guns
Beat at the steel ribs; where the blue star rays
    Burn from the welding torch and the hot steel runs
The length of a transverse bulkhead. We are the rough
    Barehanded benders of hot channel, I-beams, angles,
The makers of furnace cradles, plate hangers, tough
    Organized babies who can glory in the spangles
Of the star-spangled banner. Under some distant sky
When the gray ships go down, it is we who die.

THE REBELS

We are the ones who dissented, the losing side;
    We are the few, the trouble makers, the out-of-liners;
Too honest to keep silent, too proud to hide,
    We shouted defiance; we are the non-signers,
We are the ones assailed, raided, arrested;
    Ours is a record of promises unfulfilled;
We are the weak whom the strong have always detested,
    Unjustly tried, imprisoned, punished and killed.

We are the marchers; ours are the signs and the placards,
    The sore feet, the bruises, the indestructible hope
Of a better world. Stereotyped, labeled as blackguards,
    We embrace bullets, fire, exile and rope.
Without credit, despised, on the hard barrel's head
We lay cash blood, cold fury, and all our dead.

STEAM WHISTLE

Tall men bronzed by the sun, whose forefathers beat
    Swords into plowshares, watched from the blue hills
The chimney fires and the rolled iron's cherry heat
    Snaking the twilight. Down in the valley the mill's
Steam whistle pierced the heart as the dusty plow
    Snagged on a root, leaped, and the furrow broke
With a mighty curse for the human why and how
    Of man and beast bearing a common yoke.

Remembering the cool twilight now, and the lie
    Told by a steam whistle to the tall bronzed men,
    Are the curse and the question lifted and answered when
In the annihilation of all their hopes men die
    Far from the blue hills? And how does it feel
    Caught in these giant traps of industrial steel?

WE ARE THE QUIET PEOPLE

We are the quiet people, the ones who wait
    While others hang themselves with too much rope.
Ours is the slow tongue of patient hate,
    Silent in the cheek until some hope
Of truth appears, until some way is found
    To end deceit. The moth upon the bough,
The leaf-like worm, the snake upon the ground
    Have learned no better way than this till now.
The dangerous word, the ostentatious act
    Are not for us; ours is the quiet breath,
The hue and shade of inconspicuous fact,
    And the instantaneous flight from threatening death.
We are the weak who build brave worlds upon
The silent fang, the dust, the hope of dawn.

THE PLACE IS SURGERY

The place is surgery: the powerful light of the sun
    Pours down on the prostrate earth, on the gleaming steel.
Under this clean, blue dome brave things are done,
    For knowledge can make amends, and science can heal.
Men hold their breath while the great incisions are made,
    While rivers are clipped and the wild hemorrhages cease.
Curving through desert and plain in the wake of the blade
    Flies the hope of each that his fraction of life increase.

From valley and canyon across the prairies and wastelands
Men stitch a great shimmering lacework of water and wire.
Canal and cable are thread in their skillful hands
    And the fine drawn sutures are knotted as they desire.
Of all who have ravaged the earth, these are the first
So wisely to bind her wounds and assuage her thirst.

UNDER THE STAIRS OF HEAVEN

Under the stairs of heaven our toys will lie
Just where we left them after that hour of play
When the prize was suddenly no more worth the try,
When the game went stale, and we put the pieces away.
Spread on the yellowed papers, our toys will be
Covered with dust, just as we laid them down.
Once more we kneel on the floor, smiling to see
The bar of gold, the cross, the sword, the crown.

"With this I was rich," we say. "With this I was good.
And with these I was terribly powerful, and Oh, so proud!"
We feel the metal once more, and touch the wood,
Remembering the cries of the past, urgent and loud.
How bitterly real, how cruel, were the rules of things
When we played at bankers and priests, at soldiers and kings!

CONSTELLATIONS

The constellations beckon us each night
To heavenly heights of wonder at the way
Creation moves in flickering forms of light
That cause the mind to think, the soul to pray.

The sense of awe that overcomes the heart
Persuades the mind that there is something more
Beyond the stars, of which we are a part,
In timelessness, Creations's inmost core.

Acceptance of the going state of things
As they appear in starlight to the mind,
In turn, persuades the heart that reason brings
Tranquility when passion may be blind.
The constellations swirl in night's dark bowl
Like prayer-wheels of the mind, the heart, the soul.

HOW VERY ODD

How very odd
    To want it all
Without a God!
    How very small—
How thinking thin
    A soul must be
Standpointless in
    Eternity.

How odd to choose
    To glorify
The self, yet lose
    The awesome Why
In ridicule
    And with a breath
Make minuscule
    Both birth and death.

How very odd
    To be alone
Without a God!
    A thinking stone—
A stardust clod
    By Nature thrown
Sans wink or nod
    From the unknown.

GRACE

Beginnings are the mysteries of Creation
And Endings are the mysteries of Sense;
Between them lies the mystery of Duration
And over all the mystery of Existence;
So moves the Unknown far beyond the Known
In silent glory and magnificence
Beyond all reach, Alone in the Alone,
Forever held in one sublime embrace
Of radiant dark that beautifies the Throne
Where all else fails and there is only Grace.

SOMETIMES

Sometimes our prayers are unanswered—
    We must stay when we wish to go;
Sometimes the prize is for others—
    Sometimes the answer is "No."

Sometimes our hope turns to sorrow—
    The flowers we plant never grow;
Sometimes our love is a lost love—
    Sometimes the answer is "No."

Sometimes our effort is wasted—
    The way that is ours is too slow;
Sometimes we take the wrong turning—
    Sometimes the answer is "No."

Sometimes our will is not God's Will—
    We pray without knowing, and so
Sometimes our prayers are unanswered—
    Sometimes the answer is "No."

WHICH GOD?

The universe, conceived of as a Whole
    May be our God, as many now believe—
    A mere extension of what we perceive,
More useful to the mind than to the soul.
The plan and purpose, all creation's goal,
    Escape the tenuous webs such thinkers weave,
    Defying heights of thought that they achieve
To mock their earthly passion to control.
But others feel God's Will is destiny—
    They personalize their need in faith and prayer;
They trust God's presence and authority
    To validate the right, the good, the fair.
Which God is God, in life's extremity,
    Will give us refuge, surcease from despair?

SO MANY GODS

So many, so many
    Gods we've known!
Still, all our gods
    Are One Alone.

So many, so many
    Gods in stone!
Still, all our gods
    Our sins condone.

So many, so many
    Gods outgrown!
Still, all our gods
    Are One Alone.

SUPPOSE

Suppose that time is like a band—
An all encircling rubber band—
    Stretched to reach infinity
By God's almighty hand.

Suppose at first God made a dot—
A miracle creating dot—
    A moment of sublimity
Upon the band—a divine spot—

And as the band stretched on and on—
Revealing from creation's dawn
    All that is and yet may be—
Suppose His hand should be withdrawn.

Suppose the rubber band of time—
The strange elastic band of time—
    Stretched no more, for it had passed
The limits of His love sublime.

Suppose the band begins to close—
Contracting with creation's close—
    Suppose the end should come too fast,
Faster than the wise suppose—

Suppose creation's tiny dot
Should be no more—a vanished spot
    Of all becoming—all things past—
By time erased, by God forgot.

STANDPOINTS

To put it simply, what we see depends
    Upon our point of view, on where we stand,
Our relative position. Means and ends,
    Angles, viewpoints, all go hand in hand
With our beliefs. What pleases or offends
    May be a treacherous surface of quicksand
Beneath our feet as we aspire to view
The vista of the beautiful and true.

It well may be, the nearest we can get
    To what our minds conceive and hearts desire
Is in the standpoints that our souls have set
    To mark the heights to which we would aspire
Had we the attributes of gods, and yet
    Our limitations quench our inward fire.
Still, from some given standpoint all may find
Rewarding vistas of the heart and mind.

Our standpoint is our faith in how we see—
    Our point of view from which all things appear
In long perspective to eternity
    From what is finite, temporal and near.
Without such faith there is no way to be
    At peace with change, impervious to fear.
Standpointless, there is nothing we can trust,
No vista but the void, no hope but dust.

FAITH AND FALLIBILITY

How frail they are, these life sustaining cords,
    These value judgments of the heart and mind
That bind in action and confine with words
    The faith and fallibility of mankind!
And yet how strong! Upon a world of faces
    Turned to all who teach and preach and heal,
Who lead and dream of far-off goals and places,
    Faith fails to break the unreal from the real;
While they who weave the cords of man's unrest
    Into the bonds of trust make last appeal
To God or Nature's laws and under protest
    Confess the human weakness that they feel.
The cords that lift are also those that bind
The faith and fallibility of mankind.

HELL ON EARTH

The darkest forests of the mind invite
    Foreboding thoughts of cosmic destination,
    The fate of earth, man's self-annhilation,
The moral tragedies of wrong and right.
The artistry of mind evokes a night
    Where souls despair in dreadful expectation
    Of all-imploding, utter devastation,
Devoid of choice or chance, of fight or flight.

The heavy, ponderous burdens of the mind
    Weigh upon the spirit as a passion
        Weighs upon the cross that each must bear
        Until the light of heaven, bright and fair,
    Breaks through the trees as each one in his fashion
Sees, through faith, the hell his thoughts designed.

FAITH

Faith in a faithless world forever clings
    To all that is eternal, to the Name
That does not change with time, the Word that rings
    With meaning true, forevermore the same.
Perfection is the flower of faithful hearts
    That blooms from sacrifice for what is right;
Love is its fragrance while the day departs
    And Hope its solace through the darkest night.

Faith has no need to know why pain began,
    No need to hold all history in its grasp;
Reality for faith is God's own plan,
    And brotherhood the stranger's hand we clasp.
Life's meaning asks not bread and earthly power,
But guiding faith from hour to trying hour.

ANTI-FAITH

Anti-faith in a faithless world is born
Of inhumanity of man to man;
It is the fire, the cross, the spear, the thorn
    Of suffering since the time of man began.
Imperfection has but two ideas: one,
    To reach perfection though it be through death;
The other to pursue itself, and so have done
With heavenly hopes, with dreams and prayerful breath.

Facts are not facts, truth is not truth, but told
    Imperfect thought, allowing no defection;
Reality, though it be false, must hold
    All history in its endless imperfection.
Dialectic bound, its abstract goal
To feed the body and destroy the soul.

CHAOS

Chaos was born the instant that God yawned
    Before he fell asleep, perchance to dream,
And in that dream Creation slowly dawned
    On myriad forms that are not what they seem.
As Shakespeare said, with prescience long ago,
    "Our little life is rounded with a sleep."
A mortal dreamer, did he too foreknow
    This sleep was so divine, so sweet, so deep?
In sleep the chaos of the past gives way
    To remnant forms of mystery that involve
Creation that we have no power to stay
    Against our waking as our dreams dissolve.
Twice blest, we dream with God as he sleeps on—
When He awakens, all this will be gone.

GOD ONLY KNOWS

Where is the wind that no longer blows?
Where is the fragrance that left the rose?
Where is the water that no longer flows?
Where have they gone? God only knows!

Where is the shadow when the light goes?
Where is the light when the tired eyes close?
Where is the seed when the green plant grows?
Where have they gone? God only knows!

Where are the strivings in hours of repose?
Where are the wishes that dreams compose?
Where are the colors of lost rainbows?
Where have they gone? God only knows!

I follow the wind wheresoever it blows;
I touch the water, the seed, the rose;
I strive in the sunlight, in darkness repose;
I dream of the Rainbow that only God knows.

DOUBT

What is it plagues the mind dissatisfied,
    The heart betrayed?
Why must we crave the Absolute denied,
    The Truth delayed?

What seeks the Inmost Being of believing,
    The golden bowl
Outpouring joy, beyond the mind's conceiving,
    Of heart and soul?

What Truth Indwelling validates belief
    And calms our fears?
What is it brings our trust so near to grief,
    Our faith to tears?

In doubt we cry, yet know not why we doubt;
    From day to day
We seek the bliss that we must live without—
    Perplexed, we pray.

SACRED WRITINGS

Sacred writings, pearls of inner seeing—
    Translucent treasures of the Spirit's making
Within the living shells of earthly being—
    These are offerings for the soul's partaking.
Though there are times of thieves and desecrations,
    The pearls lie scattered wide and unprotected
On all the lands and seas of all the nations
    As if by angels strewn, by God neglected.
Yet, touch one pearl with love and piety
    And feel the Hand of Infinite Composure
That clasps the heart in safe captivity,
    As does the shell its pearl, in its enclosure.
But violate one word, one sacred scroll,
The Hand will close and crush the vandal soul.

CULTURE, IDEAS AND VALUES

Three times old Balaam smote his ass
With vicious rod and obscene word—
Three times he wronged his perverse friend
Yet had to kiss her in the end—
His eyes were opened by the Lord
And wonders came to pass.

Three times with gender, race and class
From ivory foxhole to the street
Balaam's kinfolk smite the hide
Of justice, faith and truth denied—
But still with stubborn heart and feet
Right stands with Balaam's ass.

All ye, who punish and harass
With vile distinctions breeding hate—
Look to the angel of the Lord
With lifted arm and wrathful sword!
Prepare, before it is too late,
To kiss old Balaam's ass!

OUTER SPACE

What is it now that calls from outer space
That we should come, forsaking this frail green
And fragile garden? What Deep Unseen
Remembrance calls us home from this strange place,
Engaging mind and heart to fly, to race
Into the Great Beyond? What does it mean?
What Power is here that holds our souls between
Green earth and heaven in such close embrace?

Is what is there less painful, more serene,
That we some ancient journey should retrace?
Will what is there be truthful, pure and clean
And will there be a blesséd State of Grace?
What heavenly Arm is there on which to lean?
Whom shall we meet in glory, face to face?

IMAGERY

Not to worship many images may be
    An act of self denial of a kind
That starves the soul of creativity
    And robs us of the glories of the mind.

Our courtesy and reverence paid to worth,
    Our honor and respect, our adoration
Of images of heaven and of earth
    Are jewels of life, of faith and exploration.

Our worship owes no blind obedience,
    No service of an humble, impressed heart
Beyond persuasion of experience
    When metaphysics has become an art.

With imagery we form our purest view
    Through earthly effort and divine Grace
Of what is good and beautiful and true
    And what is evil, ugly, false and base.

This is our given, and with this we strive
    Among the great creations of all time
To reach our heights, and reaching keep alive
    The vivid presence of the Most Sublime.

SECRET FAITH

How great my need to understand
When faith and greed walk hand in hand
        To reach the Promised Land.

I tremble for the faith I hold
When greed for souls and greed for gold
        Are prophecies foretold.

The power so sought was once denied
To wounded hands and wounded side
        The hour our Savior died.

How sweet the faith my heart has known
That it was love, God's Love alone
        That rolled away the stone.

I HAVE A DREAM

The fragments Nature gives too seldom fit
    The patterns of Utopias in the mind;
Too often what must be will not permit
    The luxury of dreams for humankind.

The fragments that must somehow interface
    Are of such shapes and strange variety
They often fail to find their proper place
    In ideal forms of dreamed society.

The heart in torment strives to set aside
    The differences that thwart and separate;
The mind devises ways to force or hide
    The jagged points of conflict, greed and hate.

In dreams alone, love gives the power to see
    Beyond the many to the perfect One—
In dreams alone, love heals humanity
    And fragment-grinding, at long last, is done.

THE PROPHETS

They who follow prophets, they who keep
    The faith, the true believers, converts made
    By word and deed, who die upon the blade
Of their belief—who sing while others weep,
Who march beneath the stars, while others sleep,
    To greater glories that will never fade
    From where the stake is burned, the wreath is laid
And murmuring dissent is buried deep—
All these I fear. For how am I to know
    My prophet when I hear his voice among
        The many prophets who call out to me?
And whom am I to follow? The crosswinds blow
    My heart and mind like leaves all winter flung
        To blind the path I walk to what must be.

A MALTHUSIAN OBSERVATION

A self-destructing mechanism seems
 Inherent in all things that multiply
And populate until they starve and die.
When all that sustains life has been devoured
 Or is abused—is wasted and defiled—
When Nature, spent, no longer is empowered,
 The struggle to survive grows cruel and wild.
The self-destructing passion of desire
 Consumes the treasure given by creation—
Duration shrinks as need and greed conspire
 Against extinction with mad generation.
Survival, rampant in its reproduction,
Sets holocaustal fires of self-destruction.

PSALM OF SORROW

Green pastures all have withered now and dried—
 How still the waters in a world of waste!
 How dangerous now, how deadly to the taste
Is what is left where all have starved and died!

How terrible the thirst of lives that tried
 To reach the last pure drops by drought erased!
Green pastures all have withered now and dried—
 How still the waters in a world of waste!

Weep for the Shepherd, too, who sought to guide
 His flock with rod and staff as he embraced
 The earth with love and tenderly made haste
To shield and save, to comfort and provide.
Green pastures all have withered now and dried—
 How still the waters in a world of waste!

POWER

Power is the name of the game
And it supersedes
    All else in the endless striving;
    Sheer personal power
Takes precedence over all other
Earthly needs—
    Expedient, cunning, preparing
    Through every hour.
The smallest advantage is seized
With merciless claws
    Sharpened by primitive lust
    To capture and rend;
It matters not what the goal,
The aim, the cause—
    Only the winner, triumphant,
    Exults at the end.

Yet who would resist, be the edge
Ever so small,
    To be first at the finish,
    The victor's laurel to hold,
To see his flag, his picture,
Upon the wall,
    His name in the book,
    His image in shining gold?
Look well at all men in their striving
And mark the gleam
    That burns in their eyes,
    Aflame with a power-hungry dream.

BEAUTY AND BRUTALITY

Beside his heavy chopping block
    The mighty butcher stands,
A crimson rose between his teeth
    A cleaver in his hands.

That near is beauty to the beast,
    That near is love to lust,
That near is glory to the grave
    And grandeur to the dust.

Who will be slain and who survive
    The cleaver's bloody blows?
What bleeding heart will keep alive
    The memory of the rose?

FORBIDDEN FRUIT

The story of awareness told to me
    Has left me sleepless in a world of dreams,
    Perplexed at what may mean more than it seems
To say in words about the knowledge tree.
Its fruit of good and evil may not be
    The poison fruit of ethical extremes
    But rather be what sad experience deems
The *thine* and *mine* of private property.
Awareness of one's self is nakedness
    And other-enmity, for what we own
        May never be another's to possess.
Each stands apart in God-forsakenness
    From all things else, private and alone,
        Aware that Oneness once was blessedness.

HOW MANY OF US SHALL THERE BE?

How many of us shall there be?
    The question bears upon the breath
The heartache of humanity
    In conquest, slaughter, famine, death.

The white and red, the black and pale
    Apocalyptic horsemen ride
The winds of torment and travail
    Of all who labor to decide.

Who is to live, and who shall die—
    How many of us shall there be?
This is the pain of all who cry
    The heart-cry of humanity.

All who breathe the bitter breath
    Of suffering in Gethsemane
Must choose the hurt of life or death—
    How many of us shall there be?

THE TABLE OF LOVE

The fruits of our labor are spread
On the cloth of grace
    And we welcome our friends to come
    That we might share
The bounty that God has provided
And to take their place
    At our table with joy and join us
    In thanksgiving prayer.
But they enter our presence like strangers
In little bands,
    Their bread in their pockets,
    Afraid of the ancient threat
Of alien cultures and words
They do not understand;
    They huddle together with memories;
    They sigh with regret.

Like birds who would carry their nests
In their folded wings,
    They speak of the past, and weep
    For remembered wrongs;
In the babble of tongues they laugh
At the alien things;
    They pick at our table and sing
    Their homesick songs.
Bread broken in fear is bitter,
And without trust
The bounty of God
At the table of love is dust.

ON FALLOW FIELDS

I was given food
    From someone else's hand;
Today my plow lies idle
    On the fallow land.

My cattle all are slaughtered
    By gifts from far away;
I eat the meat of kindness
    Growing weaker day by day.

I break the bread of sorrow
    From someone else's grain,
Grown I know not where or when
    With strangers' sun and rain.

My hunger was a burden
    But I was not so poor
As now I am when kindness lays
    Its shame before my door.

For I was given food
    From God knows where or why;
On fallow fields I lay me down—
    Of kindness I shall die.

THE STREET OF TEARS

Dependence is the heartache street
 That plenty shares with need—
The very stones cry when they meet
 As old wounds break and bleed.

Dependence may lead need astray,
 So seldom is it told
The hand that helps, in some strange way,
 May get a strangle hold.

The helping hand, in turn, depends
 For praise and gratitude
On need it generously befriends
 With sweet solicitude.

Each in its way, down through the years
 Both need and aid have known
The sadness of the street of tears
 That neither walks alone.

THE COMMON HERITAGE OF MANKIND

The eyes of dead men rise from watery graves
 To view again old Ocean's treasury:
Vast stores of wealth lie deep beneath the waves
 And boundless power in every landlocked sea.
Rich metals pour from great disrupted rifts,
 The oil waits pooled in prehistoric bowls,
Aquatic life survives tectonic shifts,
 The treasure grows with every wave that rolls.

So grows man's need, so grows his frenzied greed
 Upon the tides of hunger in his soul:
His thirst for power, his longing to exceed,
 His heritage of yearning to control.
It matters not which land flags are unfurled,
Who rules the waves again will rule the world.

FALSE PROSPERITY

This may be offensive
    But still a certainty—
There's nothing more expensive
    Than false prosperity.

It's a character assassin,
    A spendthrift and a thief
With fakes and flimflam fashion
    Crass beyond belief.

It's a user and abuser
    Of planet and of man—
It's a liar and self-excuser,
    Consuming all it can.

This may be hard to swallow
    But so is poverty
While the world is wont to wallow
    In false prosperity.

LEISURE

Beside the worker at his workbench stands
    The enemy of toil and worker's pride
Who offers time to rest his busy hands
    If he will only lay his work aside.
Abundant time to travel and to play
    Is promised as a child is promised toys—
Time to loaf and tinker through the day,
    Time to do the things that one enjoys.
It's not like doing nothing all day long
    And idleness need never be a bore
For one can always whistle, sing a song,
    Or just repeat whatever went before.
It's one's reward for pride and useful skill—
A gold watch, so to say, with time to kill.

THE THREAD OF REASON

The thread of reason has great strength
And nice consistency
But only midway in its length
Persuasive cogency.

Its origins of premised thought
Still seek reality;
Its syllogistic ends are aught
But not finality.

The real and rational interface
In symboled synthesis
But reach no final state of grace,
No closed parenthesis.

The mind alone, without the heart,
Threadbare though it be,
Has only ignorance for its start,
Its end, uncertainty.

SOCRATES

The Gadfly was a questioning man
Abrasive in his strife—
With dialogue, as few men can,
He edged the knives of life.

As Roman Cicero said, he brought
The heavens down to earth—
The midwife of men's serious thought
He taught what words are worth.

When earth's door closed behind him
On talk and looking-glass,
He fled where all might find him
With questions as they pass.

By force of wit and grit alone,
With hemlock on his breath,
He turned into a whetstone
Against the blade of death.

A MAN CAN BUILD A WALL

A man can build a wall against the wind,
  A roof against the rain, but words are germs
Breeding in the blood, feeding upon the mind
  In chains of phrases, in colonies of terms.
The public cup is vile with septic names,
  The printed page infected; man grows weak
With pathogenic creeds and verbal shames—
  The dearest lips are dangerous when they speak.
Words breed the plague, the fever of the brain,
  Days of suffering and untimely death;
Words swell the heart and twist the back in pain:
  The Four Horsemen ride upon man's breath.
Small wonder well men tremble when they hear
The eloquence of power—the voice of fear!

THE RICH MAN

There was a need in him to seek increase
  Of all that he possessed, and so possession
  In the end became a mad obsession
No further acquisition could decrease.
Each hour his hunger grew without surcease
  While tides of wealth flowed in without recession;
  Accumulated luxuries in succession
Glorified this need that would not cease.

So flowed the inward tide of decadence
  Upon his soul, in waves of need and greed
    That piled the flotsam wealth upon his years.
Made poor with luxury, he had no recompense
  But prayer and patience that the tide recede,
    No consolation but a rich man's tears.

CLEAN HANDS

Clean-handed scorn that seeks to denigrate
    The hard and dirty work that earns the bread
    Of labor shames us all. With faces red
We stand at garbage dump and factory gate,
At farm and mine and at the sewer's iron grate
    And beg forgiveness for the mean words said
    By haughty minded men who use the head
To hurt the hearts and hands of all who wait
Upon the Lord, brows wet with dirt-streaked sweat,
    In ways that fortune dealt and time made fast
        With daily need and life's unending cares.
Clean hands and haughty heads, lest you forget,
    You know not yet where destiny will cast
        The hard-hat crown of thorns that labor wears.

TO A ROBOT

Soulless monster of man's restless brain,
    Robot and slave, destined without free will
    To move at man's command for good or ill,
To bear his burdens without feeling pain
And when all's done to feel no joy, no gain,
    How can it be to see, yet not to see,
    To feel yet not to feel, insensibly
To die at man's command, yet still remain?

Where human hands and thoughts were once so free
    You move in chains, imprisoned evermore,
Your numbered hours consumed relentlessly,
    Your dungeon deep the sunless factory floor.
Yet this we share: what is to be will be
    And all are prisoned by a time-locked door.

PAPER PEOPLE

Once people lived in the country,
    Scratched land for their daily bread;
Now people live off of people
    And scratch city paper instead.

When they lived in the country they always
    Had something to harvest and bring;
Now they live in the city and nobody
    Harvests a blessèd thing!

When they lived in the country they planted
    Saved seed, and they saved the sacks;
Now they tramp city pavements and plant
    Paper knives in each other's backs.

Long ago they were friendly and giving
    With shelter and labor and eats,
But now they're all city strangers
    On the trash-carton, litter-box streets.

Are these the same people, these people?
    Where, and to whom, will they turn
If their paper world goes up in smoke
    And their paper lives crackle and burn?

Once people lived in the country
    Hand to mouth, hand to hand, but then
Their days were not pieces of paper
    And men were not paper men.

ROCK AND ROLL

While the music rocks and rolls
Children offer up their souls
    Enraptured by the voice and band,
    Seduced into the sorcerer's hand
By rhythms burned on lyric scrolls.

Gone are all the golden goals—
Pounding sound alone controls—
    Wild hearts race, to frenzy fanned
While the music rocks and rolls.

Lost in fields, in playing bowls,
Hearts are flesh on burning coals;
    The fiery beat devours the land
    Where helpless, screaming children stand;
The serpent crushes and consoles
While the music rocks and rolls.

SURVEILLANCE

Day and night, the glassy stare
    Of camera and computer
Watches us from everywhere
    As objects, cold and neuter.

Pick and choose, buy or sell,
    Be watery or bloody,
The glassy eye glares from its cell
    In time and motion study.

It transmits to the Bottom Line
    Where sits the Mogul neuter
Before a bright fluorescent shrine—
    The Ultimate Computer.

With entrailed numbers in display
    The beads of greed are read
As void and venal eyes survey
    The neutered living dead.

USERS

Lost are they who sink in painless sleep
    To dream inert, to suffer no complaint;
Lost are they who seek the treacherous deep
    Relieved and soothed and lulled of all restraint.
The weed, the snow, the horse, the liquid fire
    Pass from the streets across the social rooms,
Through outstretched hands, to satisfy desire
    That feels no sense of guilt or threatening doom.

Lost are they who seek the sweet release,
    The high, the low, the languid torpored hour,
The lethargy of soul that brings false peace,
    False solace, false elation and false power.
Drugged and lost, they wander through false time
On waves of self-destruction, vice and crime.

SUBWAY GRAFFITO

Let the hunger in me die!
    Free me from my slavery!
Drained of dreaming earth and sky,
Let the hunger in me die;
While my screaming veins run dry,
    Please, dear Jesus, comfort me!
Let the hunger in me die!
    Free me from my slavery!

FIRST AMENDMENT

The danger lies both in the thoughts we think
    And in the deeds our spoken thoughts provoke;
It is the thought that leads us to the brink
    Of chasms deeper than the thoughts we spoke.
Thoughts that seem so safe with rational men,
    Once spoken, leave believers in their wake;
It is belief that may destroy us when
    We take the steps persuasion bids us take.
The paths that zealots and fanatics tread
    But seldom lead the heart to what is sought;
The paths of glory weave among the dead
    Who died not by the hand, but by the thought.
Great spoken thoughts change all whom they inspire
And we who share their light must bear their fire.

HATE

The image in the mind, the blood's hot rush,
    Are nature's magic to repel the foe
With ghastly pallor and with crimson blush
    Before the struggle brings the fatal blow.
The pin-pierced doll, the propaganda spread—
    The pin, the word—are not that far apart
In seeking, safely, that the foe be dead,
    Breast pierced and bleeding, with a broken heart.
So are the mighty fallen and the weak,
    Made strong by nature's magic, put in place.
The imaged beast with severed claws and beak
    Is laid to rest in peace with victor's grace.
Thus in the mind all things man fears are killed
Before the deed is done, the blood is spilled.

THE LAW

We are a land of laws and not of men,
    So say we all—what rubbish! Laws are made
    Of ink and paper, thoughts, and hopes that fade
When practice contradicts intent, but then
There's contradiction in all things; yet when
    Self-contradiction is the charge that's laid,
    Confusion reigns, and justice makes a trade
For verdicts written with an inkless pen.

A land of morals is a ground more sure
    For good resides in human hearts and must
Support the laws or equity abjure.
Where all is change and all life insecure
    Virtuous men alone are truly just
And laws kept in the heart alone endure.

PROTECTORS

Protectors of our civil rights, what now
    Protects us from your own protecting arms?
Entangled in a web of conflict, how
    Shall we be free? Who's left to sound alarms—
To warn us of our chains and bid us hear
    The distant drums that echo over seas
From wall to prison wall, their message clear
    That we must lose, to find our liberties.

The law's frustration, born of moral doubt,
    Conflict, injustice, inequality and needs
In skillful hands turn freedom inside out,
    Forge chains of power and insult noble deeds.
Protect us, Lord, from people such as they
Who give us much, but take much more away.

THE JUNGLE HEART

The rules of law encage
  The jungle heart
Helpless in its rage
  To tear apart
Black bars of technicality
  And race to face
Concrete reality.

Primeval instinct howls
  Inflicted guilt
For the torn bowels
  Life's blood spilt
And death's finality
  Ordained and stained
With inked legality.

The jungle heart in strife
  With club and stone
Sharp tooth and claw and knife
  Strains flesh and bone
Beats bars of ideation
  Aches and breaks
Against abstract creation.

ANSWER ME THIS

Just whom, and what, and how shall we obey
  Within the scope of all we comprehend?
What is the context of authority
  Within which lies the act—the means, the end?

An act of will, beyond docility,
  May break the law, some polity offend,
Exceed permission, strain ability
  To serve a purpose justice would commend.

When comprehension reaches far domains
  Of spirit alien to the law's device
We who break the arbitrary chains
  Must be prepared to pay our freedom's price.

Our blind obedience, at its worst, sustains
    Injustice, greed, depravity and vice;
Our disobedience, at its best, attains
    A crown of thorns, a cross of sacrifice.

Imperiled, we weigh the act—the means, the end.
    Is freedom, too, bound by authority?
Within the scope of all we comprehend,
    Just whom, and what, and how shall we obey?

THE CONSTITUTION

It all was written there, or so we thought,
    On parchment pages yellowed now with age,
But time has made it clear that what we ought
    Is formed within the heart, not on the page.

Compassion cries against the rule of law,
    Equality with helpless tears is stained;
Liberty and freedom bear the flaw
    Of need to be protected and restrained.

Original intent, be what it may,
    And afterthoughts on rights be what they will,
The heart, and not the mind will have its way
    Till jurists' pens run dry and stars stand still.

Definition, logic's cornerstone,
    Enables thought to build consistency,
But vague intent and rigorousness alone
    Decry our needs, our pride, our privacy.

This document is of the heart, and though
    It bleed beneath a thousand legal knives
Interpretation has no power to slow
    The pulse that gives its meaning to our lives.

A WORD TO THE UNWISE

Rest not the soul's serenity
  On anything as frangible
As ownership of property,
  Intangible or tangible.

Rest not the mind's tranquility
  On any laws as breakable
As those that serve utility,
  The takers and the takable.

Rest not the heart's humanity
  On mortal reprehensibles
As foolish pride and vanity,
  Defending indefensibles.

Rest not the self's proprieties
  On standards as immutable
As those of closed societies,
  Endured, yet unendurable.

Rest not life's brief mortality
  On Nature's cornucopias—
On Perfect Man's morality
  In hopes and dreamed Utopias.

EQUALITY

In the eyes of God? Before the law?
Beneath the sod? In the old saw,
Between brothers, both broke,
One man's poke is like another's?

At the ballot box? At first breath?
When fortune knocks? When facing death?
In something said that was not heard?
In a book unread? A vanished word?

Where can it be, taken all in all,
This great and small pure parity—
This chainless thrall of liberty—
Fraternity—this dream we call equality?

PROTECTION

Protect me not. I will no longer pay
    The price of fear that you demand of me,
    For I am sick of my dependency
And am resolved to die in my own way.

I will not bear the terror day by day
    That drains my strength and steals my liberty;
Protect me not. I will no longer pay
    The price of fear that you demand of me.

You profit by my loss. I am your prey
    As surely as I am no longer free
    From what you say will happen, what will be
If I resist, rebel, and disobey.
Protect me not. I will no longer pay
    The price of fear that you demand of me.

CROWNING GLORY

That no man should be in bondage, my friend,
And each on his own should stand
As equal and happy as man can be—
In general, on this we agree, my friend,
That Freedom comes first in the land.

But Liberty—that's something else, my friend—
It comes with restrictions and bounds,
Permissions and powers to move, to eat,
To talk and to meet in safety, my friend—
To pray as a church bell sounds.

But our crowning glory is Choice, my friend,
In the sanctum of privacy,
Unbound from necessity's chain that binds,
To prepare our minds for tomorrow, my friend—
Our souls for eternity.

SPIDERS

Laws are cobwebs, Solon said,
    That hold the weak and helpless fast;
The strong escape—until they're dead—
    While clever spiders last and last.

Spiders multiply and spin
    Their sticky threads with tireless care;
They creep and crawl, dart out and in,
    Spinning cobwebs everywhere.

Spiders other spiders breed
    To work the webs judicially
Around the caught who stand in need,
    Who plead and struggle to be free.

When cobwebs cover earth and sky,
    And cobwebs bind the hands and feet,
When no way's left to fight or fly,
    Remembered freedom grows more sweet.

When desperate anger is held fast,
    Sage and prophet both foretell,
There often comes a mighty blast
    That blows the spiders all to hell.

RESPONSIBILITY

My risks and injuries are my own to take
    Before the law; my faults I will atone;
Who wrongs me wrongs no other for my sake;
    I choose before the bar to stand alone.
Nor will I profit by the law's redress
    If justice should be strained by biased power
To grant the commonweal unearned largess
    From treasure plundered in a black-robed hour.
I am an island in an ink-stained sea
    Of words that know no certainty or shame;
Millenniums of trial sweep over me
    In waves of precedent and argued blame;
Yet will I stand alone, as free men must,
Till islands are no more and seas are dust.

INDECISION

Dark subtleties of truth hide in the breath
    When argument is weak and fear is strong—
When change is indistinguishable from death
    And right is indiscernible from wrong.
For we are still unwilling to submit
    Our hearts to change, yet bear change as a fact;
Right or wrong, we still dare not commit
    Ourselves beyond formality and tact.
And when we would some grievous fault redress,
    Some conflict worsen, some support convey,
Our thoughts still seem too easy to express—
    Things may not be as simple as we say.
We would be less than honest then should we
Presume to say who stays and who goes free.

ONE MAN, ONE VOTE

Democracy and tragedy
    May plague the dissident
Whose less-than-half minority
    Must be subservient.

The more-than-half, the franchised free,
    May triumph for a season
Though placed in fearful jeopardy
    By justice, faith and reason.

More-than-half and less-than-half
    Rotate their powers and plagues
While oligarchs and monarchs laugh
    At tyranny in rags.

THE BIG LIE

Scream the Big Lie!
    Scream it loud and clear!
Silent Truth will die.

Scream it to the sky,
    Shrill, so all will hear!
Scream the Big Lie!

Proclaim it in full cry,
    Brazen, without fear!
Scream the Big Lie!

Allow no question why!
    In clamor far and near,
Silent Truth will die.

Soon no one will sigh,
    No one will shed a tear.
Scream the Big Lie!
Silent Truth will die.

GUILT

When wicked fires have left an ash
    And greed breaks secrecy,
Some men sell their guilt for cash
    And some for sympathy.

Some cast the ash upon the wind
    Against the smoke that smothers,
But some deny that they have sinned
    Or cast their guilt on others.

Forgiveness never satisfies—
    Guilt is the brand of Cain.
Within the heart, behind the eyes,
    The ashen stains remain.

TESTIMONY

When truth and falsity reside
    In words alone, the clever
Often brush the facts aside
    And they are lost forever.

The power of words in argument
    Persuades as it reveals
With logic what was done or meant
    But circumstance conceals.

Knowledge without words defies
    Forensic craft with silence—
Injured pride in secret cries
    When it has suffered violence.

When testimony's give and take
    Alleges without proof,
Falsehood thrives on heartaches—
    Self-interest poisons truth.

And so it goes with the accused
    As well as the accuser,
When only they know who's abused
    And who is the abuser.

INQUISITION

What we do and why we do it
    Seldom seems to satisfy
Those who would inquire into it,
    Questioning our reasons why,
And where, and when, and who else knew it—
    Upon our oath, we must not lie!

Inquisitors are devilish clever—
    First in red and then in blue,
Inquiring seems to press forever—
    Yet they ask before it's through:
Do we now, or have we ever,
    Doubted what we say or do?

Before the finding, let us say:
    Through all that makes us laugh or cry,
With doubt our reason seeks a way
    To help us live and help us die—
With both we learn, we strive, we pray—
    So help us God! We do not lie!

TOLERANCE

Too often our awareness comes too late
    In health and love and self-control enjoyed
    Before their precious blessings are destroyed
By forces of decay we tolerate.
Disease, unrest, destructive lust and hate
    Increase while tolerance still seems unalloyed
    By practices and modes, by means employed
To satisfy, exploit and liberate.
The ever present threat evolves by stealth
    Within the mind and heart, within the soul
        Of all who gain from what they violate.
In grasping imaged power, success and wealth—
    Demanding not a portion, but the whole—
        Awareness fails if tolerance is too great.

FAMILY MATTERS

How shall the law describe
    An earthly family—
A race, a clan, a tribe,
    A class of two or three?

Those beneath one roof?
    A household with one head?
Those who have no proof
    Of legal jargon said?

Those of birth unknown
    Whom misfortunes part—
Who dwell as wild seed sown
    In gardens of the heart?

Uncertain as the weather,
    How shall the law be fair
To all who live together,
    Who love and simply share?

PERSECUTION

Destroy the man! Delay to testify!
    Deny the dangerous truth that so enthralls;
    Be slow to answer when stern duty calls;
Be quick to cast a smirch and vilify.
Destroy the man! Believe that truth will die
    Upon the rack or rot in prison walls.
    Destroy the man and all he stands for falls;
Allege his every statement is a lie.
Destroy the man! Release the barbarous cry
    Of jealous power to echo through great halls
    In overwhelming waves when truth forestalls
The purposes that none can justify.
Whatever else befalls, the truth must die!
Destroy the man! Accuse and crucify!

OUTCASTS

Bare thoughts, bare bodies, bare emotions,
These
Are the trouble makers;
Unclad of all the garb they wear,
These
Are the soul shakers.

Naked truth and flesh, pure feelings,
All
Are the guilty hidden;
The good, the beautiful, the most sure,
All
Are the wild forbidden.

Adorned, ashamed, ungardened vagrants,
We
Are the born fakers;
Remembering lost innocence, unpardoned,
We
Are the image makers.

IMAGES AND PERCEPTIONS

Mistrusting every perception
    That never is sure or will stay,
Impatient of all imperfection
    Imagine this world away.

Safe in a realm of negation
    Far from earthly deception,
Dwell in the faultless creation
    Of utter imagined perfection.

Dwell with the saints and the sages
    Who found in their acts of rejection
Acceptance of infinite images
    Immaculate in their conception.

FIFTY MINUTE HOUR

Couch confession may be jolting,
Dull and boring, or revolting—
    Blighted hopes and sick despair,
Braggadocious and dolting—
    All in all, a sad affair.

Just the same, this sort of shedding,
Raveling out and time unthreading,
    Brings to light what can't be kept in—
Not unlike a change of bedding
    Tells a dream from what was slept in.

Fifty minutes may be shocking,
Couch recumbent noggin-knocking—
    Fur and feathers, such as farce is—
Past and present, sex and schlocking,
    Plot and play—but no catharsis.

Still and all, beyond a dim doubt,
Weaseling in and weaseling out,
    Self is self's own remedy.
Talk and tears, turned roundabout
    Shed insight spiked with comedy.

NIGHTMARES

That most exquisite purgatory
　Twixt anger and despair
Is oft the sleepless prefatory
　To a rare nightmare.

In that midnight desperation
　Where frustrations dwell
The past is prologue desolation
　To a splendid hell.

Embrace cold fright and perspiration
　Before the nightmares start
As prelude sweet with inspiration
　To an anxious heart.

Enjoy the furious flagellation!
　Dance on hell's hot coal!
Bizarre are ways to seek salvation—
　To purify the soul.

THE DISSEMBLER

Upon the stage of all that you desire
　You speak of love, compassion, common good,
　Social justice, family, brotherhood;
Your every word is chosen to inspire
Faith in high ideals. Your inward fire
　Shines from your eyes as if you spoke and stood
　Before your God—as if, in truth, you would
Be other than you are—a skillful liar.
The piety and virtue that you feign
　To win the approbation of the masses—
　　The simulated goodness you pretend—
Are as nothing when you fail to gain
　Your purposed prize, and as your moment passes
　　Your image dies, your canting finds its end.

THESE ARE THE DAYS

These are the days of the self-righteous
The breakers of images
Proclaiming as shams
The likenesses of gods and of men
Cherished beliefs
The icon symbols of faith
Devotion
The objects of passion and prayer.

These are the days of the destroyers
The makers of conflict
The self-appointed, the arrogant
Priests of the relative, the uncertain—
The sick generation
Of no value judgments
No adherence to standards
No refuge and no consolation.

These are the days of the unbelievers
Bereft of history
Adrift in a sea of humanity
In terror of all creation—
These are the uncivilized
The unwashed barbarians
The infinitesimally small
Primates of earth.

HONESTY

With simple courage let us lay aside
    Our crafts and occupations, our games and plays,
Our grown-up toys, our all too shallow pride
    In what we seem to others—and let us try
To find what lies beneath the things we do;
Say what we want and feel, see eye to eye,
    And sift our human substance through and through.
Let us not be actors in our imaged parts
    But what we are, down deep and underneath—
Plain folk who say straight out what's in our hearts;
    Let's bare our bones to one another's teeth.
If we be honest—if our words have worth—
We'll walk as angels on this treacherous earth.

THE FISHERS OF MEN

The fishers of men do but seine
the seas of their dreams
And the catch ingathered burdens
their ships with death—
In the chaos of yearning where nothing
is what it seems,
The nets of dominion sink empty
as sighed breath.
The banners of glory breast wind
and wave and tide
As the seas are searched for treasures
of blood and tears
By the wide-spread nets of seduction,
ambition and pride—
By the raw webbing of history,
vengeance and fears.
While wind and wave and tide
with their strengths combined
Obey the commands of nature's
inexorable Will,
They drive all ships, all nets
and the catch of mankind
Over the depths of Creation,
dark and still.
The seas of the humanity roil
through each perilous hour
That the nets are drawn in dreams
by the winches of power.

ON LEAVING MOSCOW

When glory is not glory anymore
    And citadels of dreams stare vacant eyed
    Upon the stones where heroes bled and died—
The bitter wind of change cuts to life's core.

There is no promise now, no golden door
    That valiant hearts and hands can open wide
When glory is not glory anymore
    And citadels of dreams stare vacant eyed.

Lost in the ruins no labor can restore,
    Past loyalties lie broken and denied.
    Forsaken now, on history's ebbing tide
The faithful cling to time's receding shore
When glory is not glory anymore
    And citadels of dreams stare vacant eyed.

TO A REVOLUTIONIST

Beyond the red bloom of the rose
    A time of withering will come—
Red petals all will gently fall
    And beauty now so burdensome
Be laid to rest with summer's close.

And when the winter's bleak wind blows—
    When garden paths are harsh and bare—
On withered dreams we'll walk and talk,
    Remembering, in the chill we share,
The hot sun on the red, red rose.

REQUIEM FOR SOME OLD INTELLECTUALS

To have known God and lost one's faith is terror
Beyond all terrors: among the multitudes alone
To search for other wandering souls whose error
Was brilliant reasoning, too, and a faith forgone—
To search for certainty in all things material,
Seeking the Strong Voice, destined to command,
Forswearing all that Reason deemed ethereal,
Saluting the symbols, the clenched uplifted hand.

Where now are the order and purpose the heart so sought?
Where now is the sure control of a world at peace?
All lost in a maze of terrified logical thought,
All lost in conflicting claims without surcease.
Kneel on the ashes, then, of this burned out fire;
Pray God to restore your faith and your soul's desire.

LOST GLORY

Beyond the far horizon of tomorrow
The clouds of darkness thunder as they roll!
All creation shares this planet's sorrow—
The turbulence and chaos of each soul.
The human race in anguish bears the cost
Of selfish interests with their flags unfurled—
The heart in torment cries for glory lost
That once possessed the saviors of this world.
The conflict lies no longer between classes
But between the members of each class;
How few are left to lift the helpless masses—
To aid the poor and homeless as they pass!
On fragment earth fragmented hopes and fears
Make cosmic dust of dreams, wind washed with tears.

AUTHORITY

I, who gave Authority
    Remain a prisoner of my gift;
The moving crack of light I see
    Darkens as the shadows shift.

My cell a place within the State
    And I a captive evermore
With all who suffer, serve and wait
    To hear the Key turn in the door.

No man is free—the prison wall
    Restrains both keeper and the kept;
Confinement is the lot of all—
    A bondage no man can accept.

Outside the wall Authority
    Against Authority must strive;
Within, man's lot can only be
    To keep the faith and stay alive.

All who give the gift of power
    Bear the risk of its misuse;
They who rule from hour to hour
    Bear the guilt of its abuse.

I, who gave Authority
    Made, as all must do, a choice—
Beware the State! No man is free
    Within the sound of this, my voice.

THE LIBERTY BELL

They're running away, these people!
    Didn't you know?
That's what's the matter: the steeple
    May fall, laid low
By the weight of the bell.
    They talk and they listen; they're game,
    But they're running away just the same,
They're running like hell!

They're afraid of the bell, these people!
    They're weak as water.
Gone is their trust in God to preserve the steeple;
    They feel it totter.
They're running like hell!
    In their hearts they're running, for shame
    They're running, and now they're laying the blame
On the weight of the bell.

They're running away, these people!
    Always before
They kept the faith, faith in the ancient steeple,
    But no more.
Now they're blaming the bell.
    There's no hope now of building anything stronger;
    There's no time left for the taking longer;
There's only to run like hell.

They're running away, these people!
    While the bell tolls,
While the great bright bell in the steeple
    Rocks and rolls,
They're running like hell.
    In their minds they're running for it's now or never;
    Nothing endures, they cry, nothing lasts forever;
Not God, not life, not the bell.

They're running away, these people,
    Faster and faster,
Forsaking their last best hope of earth in the swaying steeple,
    Flying disaster.
They're fleeing the bell
    Into the endless dark, and their thoughts pounding
    Are the feet of mice, ticking, computer sounding,
Running like hell!

ANGST AND SORROW

To nations as to man, the past
    Is what life builds upon,
Yet what is built can never last
    When purposes are gone.

So often when we gain our way
    It leads to angst and sorrow—
On stepping stones of yesterday
    We trip and fall tomorrow.

At such time we must regain
    The will to live, to treasure
Great purposes beyond life's pain,
    Its sadness beyond measure.

Change is the tyrant all must serve,
    Yet, dreadful as it seems,
In angst and sorrow we preserve
    The glory of our dreams.

THE WILD, WILD FLOWERS

What has become of the wild, wild flowers?
My heart cries out to know.
Where are they now, my wild, young flowers—
And where did the glory go?

Was the summer sun too much for you?
Did you quickly burn away,
Or last until fall when the deep, deep blue
Of heaven turned ashen gray?

It is win'ter now and the long, long hours
Of remembrance rest like snow
On the silent fields where the wild, wild flowers
Were blooming long ago.

ANCIENT STREET

This ancient street is now all overgrown—
Strange weeds and grasses edge the cobblestones
Worn smooth with all that they have borne and known
Of powers possessed, of deeds no death atones.

These stones have pressed the feet of legionnaires—
Here passed the glory of an empire lost.
Upon these stones strode giants of great affairs
In garments rich with gold and holy crossed.

This ancient street has felt the warmth of feet
That danced until the dawn broke heaven hued.
Here love was all and intimacy more sweet
Than rapturous dreams of sleep or solitude.

This street, these stones, all overgrown with time
Still bear a weed-flower, now and then, to say
Here passed the powerful, here the Most Sublime
Touched earth and loved, if only for a day.

IN THE ANDES

When conquerors come with horse and sword,
  With Christ and Cross, with velvet glove
To slay the past, the truthful word,
  The pride of work, the joy of love,
Cathedrals rise to praise the Lord
  Who showers his blessings from above.

But as the centuries roll by
  Cathedrals crumble, powers decay;
The conquerors and the conquered lie
  In marble tombs and common clay;
On mountain tops the vendors cry
  The wares of glory passed away.

On terraced stones the tourists hold
  Their cameras to the long ago;
With sandals, scarves and plated gold
  Down the weed grown paths they go
To disappear like stories told
  Into the valleys far below.

ASWAN HIGH DAM

Remember the slaves and weep. In a little while
  Flooding the tombs and the temples, assaulting the soul
With irretrievable loss, the dammed-up Nile
  Will blot from earth, perhaps forever, a whole
Valley of glories past. Down the flooded roads
  Empire and law, armies and gods, will be swept
In one vast debris of bodies and crushing loads,
  Music and prayer, and centuries of tears wept.

Remember the slaves and weep when the waters stand
  Still in their fury, and the moon and stars and sun
Walk night and day in anger, while the restless sand
  Swirls in the wet faces where the currents run
Against the cliffs, and where with graven smiles
Stone pharaohs kiss the feet of crocodiles.

ANTI-WAR POEMS

OUTCRY

I would speak now for all things else than we
Who speak too much. Our information drowns
Our eyes and ears and minds until we see
Nought but ourselves, and hear no other sounds
Than those we make in human desperation.

All things on earth our desperation share—
The scaly, hairy, crawling, flying things
Love life, fear death. And death is always there
In flexing joints, outcries, in beat of wings,
In fleeing terror of annihilation.

But still, to die of man's stupidity
Not knowing what has failed—in senseless wars
Of need and greed, pursued unmercifully
On land and sea and reaching to the stars—
Is death by blind, inhuman degradation.

I would cry out for all that have no voice!
And I would scream from crevice, hole and den,
From land and water, that there be a choice
Made not in madness, but by rational men
For all that lives, and for its preservation.

ROLE MODEL

He must have been survival's paragon—
That creature of the wild, now eons dead,
Who first reached out and laid his hands upon
The stone that crushed a nut, a shell, a head.
Role model for mankind, he found a tool
That would become his burden and his power
At every den and crevice, nest and pool,
To take and hold, to slaughter and devour.
With this he could protect his cave and mate,
His progeny and territorial reign—
Yet time reveals his little family's fate
When tragedy abolished his domain.
Exhumed to view are broken fossiled bones
That say his fellow creatures, too, used stones.

CONQUEST

Dissatisfied, we fan the fire
    Of ceaseless mortal yearning;
Consumed by all that we desire,
    We are forever burning.

Never have we been inured
    To ash of guilt and sorrow;
Still, hearts aflame, we grieve assured
    That we will burn tomorrow.

Grasping in our heart's embrace
    The torch of sacrifice,
We seek an earthly state of grace
    In avarice, war, and vice.

Passionately, we scheme and strive
    And ravish all we cherish,
Deserving to be burned alive
    As knowingly we perish.

ARROWS

Of all man's tools, war-signs made by his mind
    Have injured most: each movement, mark and sound,
    Like arrows shot in fear and rage, has found
Some heart, some hand, some soul, and left behind,
If not quick death by poison, still some kind
    Of memoried scratch, some never healing wound,
    Some drop of blood on Reason's hallowed ground—
No arrow yet was lost upon the wind.

On battlefields the fallen arrows tell
    Of lost beliefs, persuasions, faiths and powers;
The dead are there where martial symbols fell
    On fields of thought in never ending showers;
There crippled children wander lost, and smell
    The stench of victory in the trampled flowers.

HEART WINDS

Deep in the ash of empires
    A few hot coals remain
To start a thousand fires
    When heart winds blow again.

In every slumbering ember
    Are dreams that did not last;
The resting winds remember
    The fire storms of the past.

The red smoke clouds of glory
    Are never wholly gone;
Hot coals of song and story
    Burn on and on and on.

In treasured ash of empires,
    In memory's dark domain,
Are everlasting fires
    When heart winds blow again.

ABSTRACT NAMES

The soul inspired by abstract names
    Takes flight on Phoenix wings,
Renews itself in self-fanned flames
    And ashes of all things.

Abstract names in flames become
    The brilliant guiding lights
Of good and evil and the sum
    Of earthly wrongs and rights.

The flames give burning power to all
    The terrors man has known;
The flames shine bright when ills befall
    Man's fragile flesh and bone.

The soul seduced by abstract names,
    Impelled to Phoenix flight,
May yet leave all the world in flames
    And ash of endless night.

FRIEND OR FOE

When memory fails and who were friends are foes
    And who were foes are friends, all is in vain:
    The battlefields are flowering once again—
The flags twist with the faithless wind that blows
Men to their death. In all the world none knows
    The time or place when friend and foe, self-slain,
    Shall sleep together, ever to remain
Chameleon ash and cloud of bleeding rose.

The masses have no memory, theirs the friend
    Who last holds out the wine, the meat, the bread.
While youth, who never knew, sees but an end
    Unjustified by means; youth thinks the dead,
Part friend, part foe, died only to defend
    The faithless words their fearless leaders said.

BEFORE THE BATTLE

Merciful God, give me one tree, one stone,
    One anchor against the storm to hold me surely,
For I am less than chaff on the wind. Alone
    I am nothing. Nothing. God, hold me securely!
I beg this now while I have ease of breath,
    And lucid words remain for quiet saying;
While I am still far off from busy death
    And there is time for poetry and praying.

For it is true that we who soon may die
    Grow silent, cunning, and watchful of small things;
We memorize, and count, and magnify,
    And sometimes save our lives with twigs and strings.
God, hear me now, before I face a wall
I cannot climb, where scratching cracks is all.

THE TURNING POINT

The mightiest conflicts of the world engage
 The soul of man on battlefields of blood
Spilled both in love and hate that vent their rage
 When dreadful tides of change are at the flood.
When sorrow threatens all that life holds dear
 And life itself no longer is assured,
The conscience of mankind surmounts its fear
 And stoops to evil when cold reason fails,
When hope grows faint, yet instinct finds the worth
 Of victory more than grief that it entails.
The fires of hell burn brightest when the strife
Is for the soul of man, his loves, his life.

CENOTAPH INSCRIPTION

Pass by the ones who manufacture guilt
 From human failure, market human shame
 As if it were a product, place the blame
 Where it may not belong and lay false claim
To gardens of the heart and life's blood spilt.

Turn away from hurts and harms they vend:
 The poison flowers at requiems for the dead,
 The night-borne spiders venomous with dread,
 The mold and rot that will forever spread
Through days of retribution without end.

Pass by them now and only turn your face
 To all that clear remembrance would find good;
 Revere the brave who gave the most they could;
 In prayer be with the innocents who stood
In gardens that are now a marketplace.

GHOSTS

Out of the night sky on ghostly wings,
    Out of the clouds, the planes glide swiftly down
In twos and threes like kites drawn in on strings
    Against the blackened lumber of the town.
No tree is in the leaf, no blade of grass,
    No smoke, no wind; no live thing anywhere.
The empty streets are lakes of shattered glass
    Where broken chimneys lean upon the air.

No restless wanderer walks these streets tonight;
    Among these stones no lovers wait the dawn.
No children cry. There is no hidden light.
    Even the red pin on the map is gone.
Nothing remains but this: the guilty "Why?"
And the screams of young pilots in the night sky.

PRAYER FOR PEACE

Protect us God! Old zealots drunk with power
    Still strive to bend us to their ceaseless yearning
    That we should be as they, forever burning
With passion's flames that tempt as they devour.

For we are come to that most dangerous hour
That leads the brave to kill, the weak to cower.
    Now that our paths have reached a place of turning,
                                        Protect us God!

Upon our hearts once more Thy blessings shower
    To quench the flames that threaten our discerning.
    In peril we seek to be with You, returning
As turns the frailest leaf, the fullest flower.
With guiding Light of heavenly faith and learning,
                                        Protect us God!

CHRISTMAS EVE

The Christmas trees are dark tonight;
　　The children cry upon the stair.
In all the land there is no light,
　　No singing anywhere.

The Star of Bethlehem is dark
　　Against the gifts the bombers bring.
The pilots see no guiding spark;
　　No herald angels sing.

Upon the hills the shepherds watch
　　Beside the guns, long-ranged and strong;
But no man dares to strike a match,
　　And no man hums a song.

Fear is stealthy; fear is quick;
　　The children cry upon the stair;
The smell of pine and candle-wick
　　Is hard to breathe, and hard to bear.

COLD PEACE

The dark transactions of the time devour
　　All things. The phosphorescent slow decay
Of faith alone illuminates this hour
　　When no true fire is left to light the way.
What dreams were those of meadows bright with sun
　　And orchards snowing white upon the wind
Before the bluff was run, the harm was done,
　　And all the slaughtering maps were x'd and pinned!

These are the days men find no strength in hills,
　　No wisdom in books, no comfort in their prayer;
Their hearts are sick with fears of over-kills,
　　Electric answers, games, and poisoned air.
Under a dirty umbrella, tapes punched with tears
Make magnetic memories of these wasted years.

MIDDLE EASTERN CRISIS

Oil upon the water
  Blood upon the sand
Flow as empires totter
  Beneath the tyrant's hand.

Desert winds are drying
  Tears upon his gun
As the patriot lies dying
  Beneath the burning sun.

Planes and ships traverse
  Sky and water blue
As the many injured curse
  The powerful, guilty few.

Death's little dog awaits
  The oily, bloody bone—
He lies at heaven's gates,
  Apart, alert, alone.

REMORSE

Words alone cannot express
  Repentance and regret—
The sense of guilt, the deep distress
  That death and loss beget.

Apologies cannot convey
  The sorrow and despair—
No penalties survivors pay
  Absolve, however fair.

The frailties of heart and mind
  Bring only silent grief—
It is too much to hope to find
  Forgiveness or relief.

Remorse endures forevermore
  Where patriot blood is shed—
Nothing is as it was before,
  Remembering the dead.

THE LONG TIREDNESS

The long tiredness of the years
    Is in all things;
Too many walk the earth too close to tears
    And patience brings
No solace in a world of constant fears
    Where heartbreak sings.

The mornings wake and evenings fall
    On hours of dread;
Across the world the hungered millions call
    For peace and bread;
Sorrowing lips press hard against the wall
    Of the named dead.

The long tiredness is a blight
    And pain is prayer;
The troubled soul cries out upon the night
    Its deep despair
That ever things again should be set right
    And God should care.

THE DESERT WINDS

The desert winds will never cease to blow
    Where holy prophets once reached out their hands,
    Not for the gold that lay beneath the sands
But for the souls that avarice lays low.
When vanity destroys and empires go
    From wealth to ruin and fruitful motherlands
    Become as barren wastes where wandering bands
Thirst unto death when deep wells cease to flow.
The desert winds so merciless and strong
    Shred the palms whose branches paved the way
        For blessedness of all who dwell in peace—
Yea, for the faithful, days and nights are long
    As in their diverse ways they wait and pray
        Against the desert winds that never cease.

THE DEADLY GAME

Beneath the flag the children played
    A secret game of think and kill;
    They laughed and cried, as children will,
At what they thought and what they made.

With little minds and hearts dismayed
    At death and thinking's final thrill,
Beneath the flag the children played
    A secret game of think and kill.

A few there were who knelt and prayed
    Remembered prayers and felt the chill
    Of guilt that must be with them still,
Yet they played on, distraught, afraid—
Beneath the flag the children played
    A secret game of think and kill.

ON FOREIGN FIELDS

On foreign fields the brave are dying;
    Here at home the flag is torn.
    Many are the hearts that mourn
Faithful through the hours of crying.

On the streets good folks are trying
    To protect and yet not scorn;
On foreign fields the brave are dying;
    Here at home the flag is torn.

The dawn light breaks on brave men lying
    Far from places they were born,
    Loyal, proud, confused, forlorn
Beneath the flag above them flying.
On foreign fields the brave are dying;
    Here at home the flag is torn.

COMMEMORATION DAY

The grass grows green, the bright flags fly
On wastelands of crosses where the dead lie.
    Footsteps pass, gently and slow;
    The heart beats wildly row by row
With fear and faith that as time goes by
                                        It never will happen again.

It never will happen again! The sigh
Dies on the wind and the deep cry
    Dies in the breast; love's heartbeats go—
    Quick frightened mice under fields of snow
In their veined tunnels. The bannered sky
Overhead thunders the question: Why
    Do we kill one another? When will we know
                                        It never will happen again?

GAMES OF VIOLENCE

The dice possess no memory,
    A bullet has no friend—
None can foresee with certainty
    How violent games will end.

Their ends are often quite bizarre
    With incongruity—
Fate reaches far where chances are
    And luck is destiny.

In time, with heartsick discontent,
    The violent games are gone—
With what was meant, the bullets spent,
    The dice Death breathed upon.

AMONG THE RUINS

My spirit walks among the ruins and I
reflect
On how they came to be and how so much
was lost
To war and waste, ambition, and mad
intellect.
What pain and misery lie among these ruins!
What cost
In human suffering! Hate and greed and lust
pollute
The very dust where tyrants had their
violent hour!
These silent bloodstained stones, these empty
fields refute
The arguments of might, the eloquence
of power.

Oh, what a masterpiece divine was here
o'erthrown
Before the work was finished, dashed from the
Artist's hands
And smashed to earth as if it were a
common clod!
Of all Creation's glories that these ruins
have known
The promised best was Man! Destroyed, he
understands—
Too late—the bitter disappointment
of his God.

THE RECKLESS DEVOTION

Oh! Sailing, we're sailing
    Across the wild ocean!
Bound on the barkentine,
    Reckless Devotion!

Oh! Sailing, we're sailing,
    And drunk is our Master!
Bound for the carnadine
    Rocks of disaster!

Oh! Sailing, we're ailing,
    With cannon and powder!
Fire in the magazine,
    Worms in the chowder!

Oh! Sailing, we're wailing,
    With all parts in motion!
Seams in the barkentine
    Taking the ocean!

Oh! Sailing, we're bailing,
    And drunk is our Master!
Steering a serpentine
    Course to disaster!

Oh! Sailing, we're failing!
    We're lost in the ocean!
Lost on the barkentine,
    Reckless Devotion!

SHOOTOUT AT THE MAD CORRAL

If we stand face to face
    And aim at the head
With mutual assurance
    We both will be dead.

But if we should aim
    At the nose of each gun
With unflinching endurance
    Less harm may be done.

Our bullets might meet
    Midway in their flight—
It's the kind of insurance
    That pays off in a fight.

Let's stand face to face
    In the mucky corral
And with cool reassurance
    Assert our morale.

Let's play out our luck
    With a gunslinger's skill
And with mutual assurance
    A miss is a kill.

THE DIPLOMATS

Let the wrestlers entertain you! Step right in!
    It's the greatest show on earth! It's gigantic!
To go through life and miss it is a sin!
    It's the struggle of the century! It's titanic!
Step right up, folks—lots of room inside!
    You'll see the small made great, the great made small!
You'll see the diamond studded belt, men tied
    In granny knots, eyes gouged—you'll see it all!

Applaud the way you please, for whom you please!
    They wrestle by the rules! They know the ropes!
Peanuts! Soda pop! Help kill the referees!
    (Step up, suckers! It's your last chance, you dopes!)
Gentlemen, we give you the sport that never fails—
Those good boys from you-know-where in white ties and tails!

INTENT

It's just a matter of intent—
Not what is said, but what is meant.
That's the long way roundabout—
That's the way to wriggle out.
Let the talk be what it may—
That's the diplomatic way.

Words and substance both squirm free
Tinkered with semantically.
That's the sophistry and art
That splits a settlement apart.
That's the two-edged blade and shaft
Of the diplomatic craft.

When parties will no longer budge,
Time alone becomes the judge.
That's why things are what they are—
Why hope can rationalize a war.
That's the freedom of intent—
Not what is said, but what is meant.

THERE IS NO STALEMATE

Opposing warriors, contradiction lies
    Deep in your hearts' logic, though well you know
Your hearts are pure, and to your zealots' eyes
    The right is might as passion wills it so.
But heart opposes heart, claim cancels claim,
    And the same premise bloody purpose needs
Must serve you all: one Angel robed in flame,
    Lighting your diverse ways to final deeds.

You inspire fear, and fear the fear inspired;
    It shows in every boastful word you say.
Each weapon tested, every blast that's fired
    Destroys reason, drives true peace away.
This is no stalemate; just as it is vain
In the midst of self-made foes, to die self-slain.

STRAGEDY

Two words combine on history's crumbling pages;
    The one composed of plans and plots and schemes;
The other red with blood down through the ages,
    And both suffused with bitterness and dreams.
Dead leaders tell of strategies gone wrong
    On fields of battle, in affairs of state;
Dead minstrels weep in story and in song
    For tragedies of love destroyed by hate.

The rabble-broken statues of the dead
    Lie fallen on the crowded streets of time;
The past is prologue, as the wise have said,
    And history is the hill that dead men climb.
The *stragedy* in life is to survive,
And that in death, as well, to stay alive.

CATASTROPHE

It was the war that brought the State
    To being from democracy;
Utopian dreams were born of hate,
    Morality, hypocrisy.

Emerging vice of legislation,
    Bureaucracy and regulation,
Become a virtuous domination
    Without check or termination.

Ideals conceived to save mankind
    Destroyed themselves with moral right;
They devastated heart and mind
    With force of military might.

Duplicity and debt obscured
    Dependency and helplessness;
Unshrinkable, the State endured—
    A paradox of failed success.

It was the war, the fatal hour
    Of laws and State bureaucracy—
The vice of virtue drunk with power
    That heralded this catastrophe.

CENTRALIZED POWER

Great States are made by you and me
    From war, depression and despair.
In times of crisis, desperately,
Great States are made by you and me
Who sacrifice our liberty
    For power that only despots share.
Great States are made by you and me
    From war, depression and despair.

THE MESSAGE

Hearts and hands to fences cling
    And agonize the world to save!
    The young, the helpless and the brave
Sway the wire mesh while they sing!

While sirens scream and fire bells ring,
    While in streets men rant and rave,
Hearts and hands to fences cling
    And agonize the world to save!

Who but they the message bring?
    Theirs the message Jesus gave,
    Theirs the voice from cross and grave—
The wounded side—the broken wing—
Hearts and hands to fences cling
    And agonize the world to save!

THE PRICE OF PEACE

Who of the marchers, the placard carriers, the loud
    Singers of songs, is ready to pay the price,
The sky-high asking price of peace? Who in the crowd
    Will be first to step forward, to hunger and sacrifice?
Of all who control the world's vast tools of production:
    Stockholders, management, lenders, the endless tiers
Of executives, workers, makers of tools of destruction,
    Who will come forward? Where are the volunteers?

Who of the tax-takers, clients, the builders of debt,
    Will step out of line? Who of the chosen elect
Will be first at the window of hunger to place his bet
    On a future without war, and a world more perfect?
Who, with inflated belly, for the sake of his soul,
Will break his own, and his children's, full rice bowl?

EMPTY SHELLS

The organizations are empty,
    The causes we fought for won;
What shall we do with the empty shells
    Now that the marching's done?

Where shall we stack the placards
    And store the slogans away?
What shall we do with the anger
    That burned in us yesterday?

On battlefields silent and empty
    Old leaders speak on and on
Of the wrongs that had to be righted,
    Of things that are past and gone.

Their words still echo our anger
    But not as they did before.
What shall we do with the empty shells
    Now that we march no more?

MATRICIDE

What shall Our Father say to us
    Who murder one another?
And what will then become of us
    When we have slain our Mother?

What forgiveness shall be ours,
    Or how be reprimanded,
When we have killed all that was ours
    And come to Him red-handed?

Who is there will plead for us
    Who loved not one another?
What shall Our Father say to us
    When we have slain our Mother?

THE ANSWER

On earth no altar and no shrine
    That was not built with human toil;
They who walk on paths divine,
    Who kneel and kiss the blessèd soil
    Know the water and the oil
Marble stone and garments fine
    Are there by earthly toil and tears
    In answer to man's hopes and fears.

But war on earth and poverty
    Are with us even while they pray
For Peace with all humility—
    With memories of a darker day
    When prayers took human lives away,
When torture punished liberty—
    When holy banners, toil and tears
    Answered all man's hopes and fears.

Yet Peace on earth will come with time
    By ceaseless toil and human hand
In earthly vineyards made sublime
    By sacrifice in every land,
    By Unity all understand
Who suffer terror, war and crime.
    Peace will come with toil and tears
    In answer to man's hopes and fears.

RETURN VISIT

The forests all are gone
The lifeless seas roll on
No birds awake the dawn
    To herald the clouded sun.

The once clean air contains
Vile residues and stains
No sign of life remains
    Where poisoned rivers run.

Too many and too late
Too much greed and hate
Too few to venerate
    And now there's nothing—no one—

Only creature bones
Mountains, fields of bones—
Too many creature bones
    Revealing what was done.

BUTCHERS

Where blood was spilt and waiting to be spilt
    The butchers stand in black and bloody shoes,
Blank-eyed and cold, no consciousness of guilt
    On faces camera-shot for worldwide news.
Knives wet with human tears, they wipe the blade
    Before each throat is slashed; their cold hands stroke
The down-hung necks, and when the cuts are made
    Turn from the gush that spews like scarlet smoke.

Have you no shame, you butchers of mankind,
    Who stand stone-faced in life's fast flowing flood?
What murderous madness grips your heart and mind
    That only slaughter can assuage with blood?
Almighty God! When will the knives be through?
Butchers! Butchers! Oh, shame! Shame on you!

WE SOON MAY BE DEAD

Plow me a furrow, my true love said,
Plant me some seed for I hunger for thee.
    Not while the missiles
    Wait over the hill;
    Not while the enemies
    Plan us to kill
Will I furrow or plant, for we soon may be dead.

Dig me a deep well, my true love said,
And draw me some water, I'm thirsting for thee.
    Not while the missiles
    Wait over the hill;
    Not while our enemies
    Plan us to kill
Will I dig or draw up, for we soon may be dead.

Make me a safe grave, my true love said,
And lie down beside me, I'm fearful for thee.
    Not till the missiles
    Fly over the hill;
    Not till our enemies
    Both of us kill
Will I make or lie down, with both of us dead.

WHY MUST IT BE

My love, he was brave
    And strong as stone;
He meant the world to me.
    But he was killed, and
    Now I'm alone.
Oh God, why must it be?

My love, he was strong
    Of heart and bone;
His flag they gave to me.
    For he was killed, and
    Now I'm alone.
Oh God, why must it be?

My love, he was true—
    Had he but known
War brought no peace to me!
    But he was killed, and
    Now I'm alone.
Oh God, why must it be?

TAKE MY HAND

Take my hand, my frightened one—
    Sweet peace will come; the war will end.
    Breaking hearts must only bend
Until the storm of tears is done.

Beyond the darkness there is sun,
    All that's broken love will mend;
Take my hand, my frightened one—
    Sweet peace will come; the war will end.

So much that's good has now begun,
    Fear not the message war may send;
    All will be well, my trembling friend—
Take my hand, my frightened one—
    Sweet peace will come; the war will end.

OH BRING ME NO MEDALS

Oh bring me no medals, my brave bombardier,
And bring me no cross forever to bear!
    My heart is away where the missiles are falling,
    Far, far away where the dying are calling,
And I am heartsick with foreboding and fear.

Oh bring me no medals for me to revere;
My tears are too many, and death is too near.
    In faraway shelters the dying are crawling;
Oh bring me no medals, my brave bombardier!

Oh bring me no medals when life is so dear;
I tremble to lose you, I tremble with fear.
    My heart is away where the missiles are falling,
    In far away silos where you may be calling
And I cannot help you, or hold you, my dear;
Oh bring me no medals, my brave bombardier!

OH SING ME NO WAR SONG

Oh sing me no war song,
No war song so brave;
Oh sing me no war song,
Or weep o'er my grave.
But sing me a peace song,
To heaven I go;
I would go with a peace song,
Sing it gentle and low.

For I was a stranger
And killed in a fight;
Oh I was a stranger
Who passed in the night.
I was caught in the cross-fire,
I could not get out;
And I died without knowing
What the fight was about.

Oh sing me no war song,
For I was not brave;
And I'll never rest in
A brave fighter's grave.
But sing me a peace song,
To heaven I go;
I would go with a peace song,
Sing it gentle and low.

THERE'S NO ONE TO TELL

Come home, my lover, wherever you are,
Come home from the battlefield, home from the war.
    Come to my arms and lie down by my side,
    It's all over now and the gunfire has died;
The white ash is blowing where hot missiles fell—
There's peace in the world
                    but there's no one to tell.

Come home, my lover, wherever you are,
Come home from the battlefield, home from the war.
    Come to me now for I search everywhere,
    I call into space, but no one is there,
For all of us perished in our underground hell—
There's peace in the world
                    but there's no one to tell.

Come home, my lover, wherever you are,
Come home from the battlefield, home from the war.
    Come to me now, for I blow with the wind,
    A flake of white ash where the war map was pinned;
If you could but hold me close, all would be well—
There's peace in the world
                    but there's no one to tell.

STORIES

WHOM GOD HAS TURNED AWAY

Close by the cattle loading chute
A stone's throw from the railroad track,
Righteous tongues have cast their spell
Upon a bare, clapboarded shack.
Inside its walls, so people say,
Live those whom God has turned away:
Sweet Tamarac, the maniac,
Fair Lacybell, the infidel,
And Maude, the mute.

On evenings when the dusk is warm
Fair Lacybell goes down the streets
To wreck the kingdoms of the blest
And give her light to men she meets.
Sweet damozel, pale girl of sin,
Fair Lacybell, she takes them in
And gives them sweets in dark retreats;
Then thinks it best they be confessed,
If possible, from harm.

But Tamarac has not come down
To earth these many burning years;
Her brain afire, the throb and swell
Of flames has put an end to tears.
The story goes that there was one
Who loved, and left her so undone.
Through wildest fears, his voice she hears,
While Lacybell, the infidel,
Her sister, roams the town.

Down by the cattle loading chute
One stormy night, some nine years back,
In frenzied loneliness of hell
Was born a child to Tamarac.
These are the three whom people say
God turned away:
Sweet Tamarac, the maniac,
Fair Lacybell, the infidel,
And Maude, the mute.

THE SYCAMORE TREE

There's a sycamore tree in the canyon
And a new rope I bought in town:
    There's a sycamore tree
    Where I'm gonna hang me,
But who's gonna cut me down?

I've been a drifter and I've been bad
Passed up the good breaks I might've had;
    Now I'm gonna hang me
    From that sycamore tree,
But who's gonna cut me down?

Well, I've lied and I've cheated
Been false to my wife;
I've wasted love and I've wasted life.
    Now I'm gonna hang me
    From that sycamore tree,
But who's gonna cut me down?

A little brown dog without any brains
Tried to stick with me but couldn't hop trains.
    Now I'm gonna hang me
    From that sycamore tree,
But who's gonna cut me down?

Well, I've roamed and I've rambled
Around all of the bends
And I've been to bed with the wives of my friends.
    Now I'm gonna hang me
    From that sycamore tree,
But who's gonna cut me down?

There's a sycamore tree in the canyon
And a new rope I bought in town;
    There's a sycamore tree
    Where I'm gonna hang me,
But who's gonna cut me down?

THE TIN SHOP

It was on a warm May morning
With my lunch in a paper sack
I went down to the Mississippi,
And friend, I never looked back.

I was going to work that morning,
That warm spring morning in May,
When I smelled the smell of my tin shop
More than a mile away.

I smelled the smell of the torches
And of acid eating on tin;
I heard the hiss of the soldering irons
As they burned the solder in.

When the bus doors opened and closed
I felt the clash of the shears
Slicing the bright new sheets of tin,
And the sheets of tin were years.

All the spouts and gutters and drains,
All the tin-roofed town,
Clattered and crashed as the mallet
Of sunshine beat them down.

Clattered and crashed and crumpled
And twisted and curled
In the soft warm wind of that morning in May
That changed my world.

I got off the bus and hoofed it
With my lunch in a paper sack;
I went down to the Mississippi
And never once looked back.

The Mississippi is wide, my friend,
And deep as deep can be,
Drifting its way, as I drift mine
Seeking the deep of the sea.

PENELOPE

Penelope Gray one winter's day
Sold both her cows and went away;
Put out her fire and locked the door,
Let down the pump, and nevermore
Set foot inside the neighborhood.
She left for good; they knew she would—
She had her pride.

A shameful thing! Back to the spring
They counted fingers, felt the sting
Of adding nine. Yet all they knew—
The two and two made less than four—
Gave not a clue
To who he was, or where she went,
Or whether she was called or sent,
Or if she cried,
Or whether she was bitch or bride.
No, not a clue.

And so the doubt, the dreadful doubt
Remains about
Penelope.

TO A LATCH UNLIFTED

There is a hand would lift the latch for me
If ever I should chance to pass that way,
By such a well-filled lamp as hers I'd see
Things different, but I wonder, would I stay?

There is a pillow white beside her own,
And there is much that we could do and say,
But could I let the wind pass by alone,
Or die enough to be content to stay?

They say that bread will strangely turn to stone
When hearts are hungry for the road or sea.
And I have heard how bitter and alone
A man beside a well-filled lamp can be.

THE RETURN OF THE POET

This is the street, and these are the solid houses;
    These are her neighbors' faces.
O tell me, was this what she had in mind
    When she spoke of the dreamed-of places?

Are these her brood, lined up like birds on the curbstone,
    Mysteriously watching the gutter-stream?
That step at my back—is it his? And this—
    Is this what she meant by her dream!

Soiled little urchins, our heaven lies in that gutter;
    Ours and a million others.
Remember this hour—a wandering poet was with you;
    Remember tonight—and whisper it to your mothers.

OLD BOOKKEEPER

For years you have lived
Behind this desk;
Each day you have made your entries
And footed the columns.

Now they are changing
The system.
A new face has looked at your old journals
And laughed.

The new face does not know
This blot of ink
Is what remains of despair—
That this erasure
Followed a vagrant hope
In the gray procession
Of your yesterdays.

The new face does not know
This new system
Too, will sometime be
Shredded papers
And memories.

ESTRANGEMENT

A shut door—but a shut door doesn't end it;
It goes on, and the mad days send it
To watch at the window and to listen
Where the traffic rattles and the streets glisten.
The nights send it away muttering
Words that burn, like a candle guttering,
Something about not coming back. Violently
Things go out and creep back silently.

A shut door—one on either side of it.
That doesn't end it; a door doesn't hide it.
It's the cups unwashed, the things not mended,
The burned table's edge where the cigarette ended;
It's the unpaid bills and too much drinking:
The over-drawn effort to keep from thinking
Something that's got to be thought completely—
Washed and ironed, and folded neatly.

A shut door—and the house divided aches
With the endless time a footstep takes
In the distant room. Again the key turning
Clicks through the mind, and the night's yearning
Melts into shame: all the shabby arrangement
Cheapens the reason, the hate, the estrangement.
A tense hand gropes for the night-light, snatches
The fresh cigarette, the tattered matches.

THE GAMBLER

He gambled with a wife,
A pistol and a knife;
    He'd bet on anything
    At table, track or ring,
And he'd back a gut-felt hunch with his life.

To him death was a game
And he played it as it came;
    While a hustler held his head,
    With his parting breath he said,
"I'll bet the House and Odds will be the same."

PURITAN AFTERNOON

They sat apart and watched the slanting rain,
The wild, persistent downpour of the rain
That held them prisoned. Neither now could go
And neither dared to move. Defeat might show
In the lifting of a hand, or breathing faster;
A toe tapping the rug might bring disaster.

Drop followed drop against the widening stain.
She might have got a rag, sopped up the rain;
He might have stayed the torture with a word,
Coughed, or moved a chair. Yet to have stirred
Had brought them nearer, threatened and diminished
The overwhelming sense of things finished.

The splash from gutter spout to foaming drain
Pounded the frayed senses, teaseled the brain.
He would not look at her, nor she at him;
They sat watching the window with faces grim,
Edged with lightning, while the serpent of long thunder
Writhed through the sky and circled them, over and under.

ELMER INZER

Elmer Inzer's eyebrows always lifted
    At the ordinary dust that things collect.
In the art of devastation he was gifted,
    And he moved as one cerebrally elect.
He'd run his finger over things we loved
    And find a lump in any chair he sat in,
For Elmer always came to us white-gloved,
    And Elmer always thought of things in Latin.

He'd lift a cover's edge and peep between
    And put it down again to save our feelings,
But in a glance we knew that he had seen
    Our soul's swill of ditch water and peelings.
He died with our ten fingers on his throat
In the middle of a simple "Quote...unquote."

BROKEN WINDOW PANES

The broken window panes
    Cry where the heart was thrown:
        The smash and crash
        The room in trash
    The wreckage of a bleeding stone
Love's scattered last remains.

The curtains lash and lash
    With thongs of morning sun:
        White walls torn bare
        Black nail holes there
    Hold darkness of the night's rage done
Crushed cold and burned to ash.

The wind through vacant eyes
    Implores the nevermore:
        The lost and gone
        The dreamed upon
    Love's remnants shredded on the floor
Love lost in paradise.

THE MISANTHROPE

A lonely man, indeed, was he
    Who hated all mankind—
Who only saw hypocrisy
In civilized society
    And perfidy of mind.

The flowers of evil bloomed within
    His solitary heart—
At war with every vice and sin
From all to whom he was akin
    He held himself apart.

Alone in his disgust, his scorn
    Of mankind made him seem
A creature wretched and forlorn—
Ridiculous, while he was torn
    To ribbons by a dream.

THE PAINTED DOOR

The name, the street, the room
Gone with time
Instead
Only the rain
The steep stair climb
The hallway gloom
The afternoon
Remain.

These, and soon
The painted door
The bed
The porcelain stain
Before
And after
Laughter
These remain—

Warm perfume
In the rain
Where ghosts have lain
Entwined
Beyond the gloom
Behind
A painted door.

SECRET

Should we be left alone
    Our two mates dead,
Let us come together
    For we love, we said.

And so we lived our lives
    To others true;
We never spoke again
    What we might do.

Now they to whom we gave
    Our loves live on
And what was ours is lost
    Now you are gone.

THE VOICE

A voice calling
At the wrong door
A wrong voice
Answering
The silent retreat
The caller
Unknown.

Remembering names
The listener
Tense, cautious
Searches among old fears
For vanished loves and hates
Unearthing one.

The caller called
From the open doorway
Becomes the listener
Turns away
Torn by the two mistakes.

THE LOVE LETTER

It wasn't one of mine, you know,
And yet he somehow laid it so—
So—
What shall I say?—so placed
Upon his table
So open-faced
In passing I'd be quite unable
Not to know.

Perhaps I should have been concerned
More than I was at what I learned—
Turned—
How shall I say?—his tender
Into words
And render
Truth to all the over-heards—
Of course, I yearned—

But now the letter's somehow gone
It's penance perfume lingers on—
On—
How shall I say?—the fireplace
Smells of love,
Perfumed, old lace
In ashes—the burned flowers of
The dead—the gone.

I'm pleased he finally did agree
To let himself return to me—
You see—
How shall I say?—I'm lonely,
If you will,
Being only
One of two—yet lonelier still
As one of three.

IN A CONVENT GARDEN

I search your face to find the changes there
    That time has made; each faint or furrowed line
Will tell me how it's been with you somewhere
    Since last your hands were tightly clasped in mine.

Your eyes will tell me what your heart has known
    Of faith and grief, how many tears you've shed
For others' suffering that you made your own,
    Restraining sorrow, sharing hope instead.

Your lips will tell me all the words you've breathed
    In tenderness, perhaps impatience too;
The lines around your mouth are treasure-wreathed
    With memoried prayers, as I remember you.

I search your face to find the long ago—
    A passion flower the vines of time entwine—
And as I hold your gentle hands I know
    Deep in your heart you, too, are searching mine.

POTPOURRI

THOUGHTS

Full of quirks
The mind works
Steady by jerks
Jostles and irks.

Words and ink
Garble and kink
Shrivel and shrink
Thoughts we think.

Nevertheless
In wretchedness
Thoughts do express
Our knowingness.

PERSPECTIVES

A sated ape in a cage, fingering
The curved bits of a broken bowl,
Holds piece to piece
And feels a lingering
Urge to create
In his primate soul.

A hungry ape in a cage, quickened
With fear and anger, is soon through—
Forgets creation,
And screams his sickened
Primitive terror
Across the zoo.

BAD LUCK

When everything we hoped for
Fails
And every gain has turned to
Loss,
It makes us wonder
Where and when
We shot the albatross.

THE DROPOUT

The urge to be profound
    Is always such a grind,
So mostly I just hang around
    On corners of my mind.

I take whatever comes
    Along with loaves and fishes;
I like to watch aquariums
    Of wiggly words and wishes.

I'm partial to truth fairies
    Who endlessly explain
The jabberwocky libraries
    That rattle bone and brain.

Occasionally temptation
    Brings a lazy sigh
As the marvels of creation
    Slut and slither by.

It's like the lost and found
    Department of the Store
Where the dropouts hang around
    In limbo evermore.

RESEARCH AND DEVELOPMENT

As we progress with R & D
  We may, as we experiment,
  Implicate and implement
A dire catastrophe.

Tempted by the tools we own,
  Our tinkering with the universe,
  Time may tell, could be far worse
Than letting it alone.

Love of knowledge and of wooing
  Truth as ideal, chaste and pure,
  May give us ills we cannot cure
And be our life's undoing.

Before we leap beneath the covers,
  Eager as a passionate youth,
  History warns us abstract truth
Has tricked a world of lovers.

GOTCHA!

Before you answer, think twice—
Two nasties never make a nice.

Nasties spoken, trouble starts—
Silence broken, breaks hearts.

But silence kept by one, please note,
Is rope around the other's throat.

BABEL

The tower that was a tower
Is now a sphere;
The land of Shinar
Where we are
Is here
And power no longer power.

The word that was the word
Is now a sound;
The voice, a ram's horn,
Cries forlorn
The world around
Heard, yet still unheard.

The rod that was a rod
Is now a wand—
The conjurer's stick
Before the trick
Of death beyond
A God no longer God.

ARGUMENT

In argument we often find
Before we leave our wits behind,
That he who has an axe to grind
Would split our skull to change our mind.

It's better far that such as we,
With cowardly tact and courtesy,
Should praise the edge of cutlery
To save our skull and sanity.

BEYOND SLEEP

Thoughts cross the mind
    On sleepless nights
Like lightning bugs
    And meteorites.

The little gray cells
    Watch them die
Like fireworks
    In blackened sky.

When morning comes
    With yawning dawn
All that remains
    Is what is gone.

TODAY

Today is really not today,
    Not Tuesday, I'm quite sure.
I think it might be Saturday;
    It's really quite obscure

How any day, but not today,
    Could be today at all,
Yet I'm convinced it's Saturday
    And something will befall

Ahead of time and out of sync
    With earth and moon and sun;
The continental shelf might sink
    Or rivers backward run.

Who knows what happens on the days
    That aren't what they should be?
Maybe they are all the days
    That never were, but could be.

Where what is when I don't much care
    And yet I'd love to know
If this is Saturday, then where
    Did Tuesday have to go?

CHIMERAS

Imagining is always chancy—
    Passing a familiar face
A frightful, idle, foolish fancy
    May disrupt the commonplace.

It may be neither male nor female,
    Or what's worse, it both may be—
A lion-goat with serpent's tail,
    A monster sexed angelically.

Chimeras lurk where least expected—
    Grotesque gargoyles, unreal creatures
Spouting from the most respected
    Plain and ordinary features.

Take care, beware, when fancies frolic—
    Sense and sanity forsaking—
Madness is a dreamaholic
    Savage drunk with image making.

THE SUDDEN WORD

It is like running against
    A wet cobweb
    In the night—
The things you said
    Come back to me
    So unexpectedly.

VACATION

Any time you think you know her
    Take a woman out of context
But beware the games you show her—
Any time you think you know her
She may call the marks you owe her—
    Leave you tapped out and perplexed.
Any time you think you know her
    Take a woman out of context.

ESCAPIST

I blew an amber bubble once
    Of silver and of sin
To shut the world without me out,
    The world within me in.

It was so large and beautiful,
    So marvelously thin!
And then there came a snooping saint
    And poked his finger in.

EXPRESSION

You wove your fragile song against the skies—
The filmy gossamer web the spider weaves—
While I, who could not fly, made silver threads
And tangled them among the rotting leaves.

THE BLUE TEACUP

Once when I was preparing my things;
Once when I was going on a long journey,
Someone came and slipped into my hand
A little blue teacup.

I have never seen a teacup so frail;
I have never seen a blue quite so wistful,
And yet I did not pack it with my things;
It was absurd that I should take a teacup.

WHEN I HAD DROPPED THE WELL-ROPE

I saw myself, above the mossy brim,
Leaning through the blue disc of the sky—
A little figure in a tiny heaven
Miles above the thing that I desired.

DREAMER

A little boy
In overalls,
Ragged at the knees,
Picking violets
In the sunshine
Among the heaven trees.

SCHIZOPHRENIA

"The world is mad," the aye-aye said
    And hopped upon the last car
Of a train inside his brain
    And went to Madagascar.

FAILURE

We stood in the dry channel
Of an ancient river
Speaking of failure.
I saw
A thousand dams
Beneath the silt
And at each turning of the way
A hidden rock.

CURIOSITY

To love a thing and yet not know its name
Need never bring regret or be a shame
When knowledge comes with tearing things apart
And thrusting knives into a beating heart.

THE BANQUET

I will not go
To my friend's banquet.
My friend
Is a stranger
When he divides himself
Among his guests.

TEA FOR TWO

How long will the water boil
    Before it boils away?
A cup of tea for you and me—
    Please, please stay.

Will you have it weak or strong?
    Better have it strong.
Outside the wind is bitter cold,
    The afternoon is long.

A cup of tea for you and me,
    Brewed of an old desire;
The fragrant smoke of lemon rind
    Upon an open fire.

IN EARLY SPRING

No one saw
My love and me
Shaking apples
Off a tree.

When we bent
The tree-top tall
No one heard
The apples fall.

That's because
In early spring
No one thinks of such a thing.

SURVIVAL AT THE SINGLES BAR

Some wild, untamed, primeval thing
  Moves deep in me, and while you speak
The coil, the venom, and the sting
  Prepare for you inside my cheek.

For you who look at me this way
  Would tear my flesh and bones apart.
Like any hawk that kills a snake
  You'd like to feast upon my heart.

Frozen-eyed, you raise your glass,
  And I lift mine—it's all so cool,
So velvet soft—like slithering grass
  Beside some green, infested pool.

DYING ECHO

We have emptied ourselves
  To one another,
Our conversational cup
  Is drained.

Though our talk was open
  And unrestrained,
So little there was in the cup
  Of what remained.

  Lip stained,
  We hug and stand
Clasping still the empty cup
  Hand in hand.

THE LISTENER

The falling tree
    The sorrowing word
    That no one heard
Reach out to me.

My soul is stirred
    By mystery
    Anxiety
At what occurred.

It must not be
That heart and tree
    Should crash unheard
So silently.

HYPOCRISY

How would we ever get along
    Without polite hypocrisy?
With so much right and so much wrong
How would we ever get along
Without pretending weak is strong
    And pretty hands make perfect tea?
How would we ever get along
    Without polite hypocrisy?

MIRAGES

A desert mirage
    Is Nature's way
Of turning seeable
    Hot air to play
    Or parched dismay,
Depending, thinkable or unthinkable
    On what the seen
    May mean,
Whether, in fact, it's drinkable or non-drinkable.

Another mirage
    Is Nature's way
Of turning unbearable
    Doomsday
    To hearsay,
Apprehending an insufferably terrible
    Obscene
    Foreseen
Holocaust as, in fact, shareable or non-shareable.

SHARING NOTHING

The sadness of
Equality
Is to have
But not to be.

Still, when heads
Begin to fall
To have and be
Is worst of all.

Best not to have
And not to be
Sharing nothing
Equally.

SLOW MOTION

Sometimes at night I have a notion
    Things are stranger than they seem.
Daily life is in slow motion
While in hours of deep devotion
Time accelerates its motion—
    All becomes an instant dream.
Sometimes at night I have a notion
    Things are stranger than they seem.

SMELLS

Boys should smell of exercise,
    Hot animals and leather,
    Of piney woods and weather
And of smoke that burns the eyes.

Girls should smell of mysteries,
    Strange exotic incense
    Brought at very great expense
From far Antipodes.

When exercise would be too funny,
    Lap-robed in their motor cars,
    Old boys should smell of good cigars,
Of brandy and of money.

When mysteries, like birds, have flown,
    Prayer books on their knees,
    Old girls should smell of memories
And delicate cologne.

LITTLE WINGS

I let alone the things that I
Can miss without a porcine sigh—
    The noxious things—I set my will
    Against the common kind of swill
Tainted, spoiled, a little high.

Some things are just as well passed by,
Although I'm tempted just to try,
    But things I'm sure will make me ill
                                        I let alone.

Although in mud I sometimes lie,
A pig with little wings am I
    Who grunts along to butcher's kill;
    I know that pigs don't fly, but still
What smells more of the sty than sky
                                        I let alone.

MOTHER NATURE, FATHER TIME

Mother Nature, Father Time,
    Have grown too old to clean and care—
Their house is deep in dust and grime;
    There's something worn-out everywhere.

They don't pick up what's left behind—
    They just ignore it, or what's worse
They just forget, and don't much mind
    What happens to the Universe.

That's the way it is with old folks—
    Dust is stardust, grime sublime—
It's best to laugh and crack old jokes
    With Mother Nature, Father Time.

BITTERSWEET

When our bellies start to bag
And our faces tend to sag—
When we're limper than a rag
And we whimper and we nag,
Lift the head to touch the ceiling,
Find a smile that is appealing,
See an image sweet and healing
From a bygone youthful feeling.

It isn't all that hard, you see—
Now when you turn and smile at me
And I smile back, you must agree
We're quite the way we used to be.
But if we're only just pretending
Youth and love are never-ending—
If all we see is what's past mending,
Empty smiles can be heart rending.

SEXOLOGY 101

He is he and she is she
(Speaking tautologically)
But he is she and she is he
Expanded out
Without a doubt
Symboled sociologically
Equated dialectically
Rhetorically
Asexually
Illogically
Bogs the mind
Of all who grind
The grist of rationality.

SAFE SEX

Sex closets all are plundered—
    There's nothing more inside.
We wonder if they blundered
    To open doors so wide.

What's under skirts and breeches
    Isn't secret anymore—
We've learned what science teaches—
    We're more active than before.

Our worries and diseases
    Are public as the street—
When we play as fancy pleases
    We are careful, clean and neat.

It's a risky, rolled up curtain—
    It's tricky as fresh paint—
It's nice and safe, we're certain,
    But surprise! Sometimes it ain't.

COSMIC MYSTERY

Something always puzzles me
    And Nothing even more—
Of all Creation that I see
Something always puzzles me
That what is here should ever be
    Where Nothing was before.
Something always puzzles me
    And Nothing even more.

ON NOT DRIVING ANYMORE

When your eyesight's a disaster
    And you have a tin ear
And you can't fare any faster
    Than you can see or hear
It's time to get a chauffeur
    Take a taxi or a bus
Or to walk or get a gopher
    Who will fetch without a fuss—
It'll be more fun to fiddle
    With the perks of your distress
Than be mashed up in the middle
    Of a fender-bender mess.

LIMBO LAND

In Limbo land there is a tree
Where monkeys play eternally.
    Outside the gate of Heaven's zoo
    That only lets the chosen through
They swing and chatter, wild and free.

As far as any eye can see
The green tree stretches endlessly
    For monkeys skies are always blue
                    In Limbo land.

It's not their fault that they should be
Sequestered through eternity.
    Safe from Hell and Heaven too,
    Monkeys do what monkeys do
                    In Limbo land.

SMILING TRANQUILITY

Confused and confusing
  As things may be,
Amused and amusing,
  It seems to me
Is better than refusing
  To hear and see.

Acceptance and accepting
  Of the adverse,
Expectance and expecting
  Things to get worse
Is better than rejecting
  The universe.

Beguiled with the beguiling
  Through the years,
Reconciled while reconciling
  Faith with fears
Is better done with smiling
  Than with tears.

CODES, PUZZLES, ENIGMAS

Is it so meaningless to ask
  What lies beyond the bounds of wonder?
While breaking codes is thinking's task,
Is it so meaningless to ask
What lies behind grim Nature's mask—
  Beyond the power of mind to plunder?
Is it so meaningless to ask
  What lies beyond the bounds of wonder?

GROWN UP

Geez! What fun it is to see—
    When others think us dumb—
Beyond ourselves, in fantasy,
    To what we may become!

A ball glove, bike, an old guitar,
    Street slang words that annoy
Make them think that's all we are—
    If we are born a boy.

A rag doll, lipstick, bangs and friz,
    Ungraceful slump and curl
Make them think that's all there is—
    If we are born a girl.

They never guess what's going on
    Behind our sulky eyes—
That we're grownup, goodbyed and gone,
    World famous, rich and wise.

CAUSES

There are two sides to every coin,
    Or so the saying goes—
Remember, when you're asked to join,
    The thorn goes with the rose.

Old saws like these are somewhat worn
    With use throughout the years—
But sharp of tooth when flesh is torn
    And coins are wet with tears.

OLD CLOTHES

Old clothes deserve a mention
When speaking of the real—
They never call attention
To how comfortable they feel.

Like friendships of long standing
A little worn with wear,
They never come demanding
Extraordinary care.

They slip on in the morning
And know just where to go
In their habit of adorning
For service more than show.

At evenings they are laid by,
To rest from wear and tear,
With careful mending made by
A good hand here and there.

Old clothes are had the hard way
Of wear out—make it do!
They are anchor, sail and mainstay
Of the tried against the new.

SUPERIORITY

Manners say too little
And morals say too much;
The one is shine and spittle,
The other vague to touch.

But a fit and proper conduct
With a true genteel interior
Is a decent sort of construct
To make a man superior—

Not to other men or fashions
In bitter social strife
But to vicious pride and passions
In the market place of life.

WATCHES

One was a ticky one, alas—
    A real stem-wound, old fashioned piece
    With balance wheel and chime release—
With solid gold-cased works of brass.

The other was of modern stripe
    That never needed to be wound—
    With crystal quartz that made no sound—
The bejeweled, digital, battery type.

The odd thing was that neither one
    Knew what time it was it told,
    And as the two of them grew old
They never knew what they had done.

Their spring and battery both gone dead,
    They went where all things stop and start—
    With time that dwells within the heart
Unfalsified, untold, unread.

STRING

So much is like a ball of string,
Knots and all, from everything
That came wrapped up with it and tied
To keep its goodies safe inside.
It seems a very curious thing—
All that's left is wrapping string.

THE ACT OF GIVING

The sweetest gifts are given
Secretly
The purest prayers are said
Anonymously
The thankless love
The silent grief
Escape the ever present thief
That steals conspicuously.

Not to expect is truly
To be free
To give without request
True charity
The gentlest way
Is always best
When gratitude is laid to rest
In quiet privacy.

FOR SALE

Gone is all the happiness—
    The house is deathly still—
The flowers have died of loneliness
    Along the window sill.

The cat is curled upon a step
    That no one steps upon
To sleep away its helplessness
    Now everyone is gone.

Of all who live in houses
    How few there are who stay—
The trash barrels of a lifetime
    Wait in the alleyway.

The dry leaves of remembrance
    Eddy as they fall—
The wind sweeps scraps of bitterness
    Against a concrete wall.

NEURONE SOCIETY

Suppose you were a neurone,
    A complicated process
In some tidy Giant Brain
    Devoted to man's progress.

You'd extend your dendrites
    To get more information;
You'd reach out your axone
    With charged anticipation.

You'd pass along the input
    As busy as can be;
You'd be a useful member
    Of neurone society.

You'd dwell within the Big Brain,
    A minuscule conjunction;
You'd never have to act beyond
    Your input-output function.

You'd never have to be alone
    Or think a thought clear through;
What went on in flesh and bone
    Would never trouble you.

And if the Big Brain suffered
    Cerebral inflammation
You'd die a wild synaptic death
    Of crazy information.

THE LITTLE HILL

I stood upon a little hill
And scratched whatever itched until
I noticed much to my dismay
That I had scratched myself away.

I think the fire ants on the hill
Upcrawled and nibbled me, but still
I never knew just which was which,
The ants, the scratching, or the itch.

I know I kicked the little hill
And itched and scratched and kicked until
I noticed I was finally free
Of ants and itch and scratch and me.

THE INNER CIRCLE

Beyond the natural forces, weak and strong,
    Electromagnetic
    Gravitational
    Perhaps a fifth
There is one more that unseen moves along
    The enigmatic
    Conversational
    Myth and kith
Of intricacy to which but few belong.

Within the force-field of the elite, known
    Circularity
    Blasé and casual
    Pins and spins
The erudition of its own renown;
    Peculiarity,
    Brash and sensual
    Whims and sins
With arrogance contrived for effete put-down.

So are the forces of the world aligned
To move all things and disarrange the mind.

SUPERASYMMETRY

The ultimate catastrophe
    From which there's no recovery
In natural philosophy
    May be the dire discovery
That unified reality
    Is supermathematical
And all dimensionality
    Is superasymmetrical.

But something so acataleptic
    Bakes no bread that's eatable
By empiricist and skeptic
    Who doubt the unrepeatable.
The ultimate catastrophe
    May leave the world unshaken
And, speaking metaphorically,
    The bread half baken.

CROSS-TOWN

Broken locks and broken doors
    And blood upon a knife,
Broken stairs and broken floors,
    Outside, a broken life
Bleeds on the steps as pimps and whores
    Beat down an angry wife.

Cross-town, sparkling limousines
    Glide down the broad parkway
Between the shops and holy scenes
    With stereos that play
Sweet Christmas carols to philistines
    And Christ, to make his day.

VISION

Not all see clearly in the light
    And some see only what is near;
Some multiply what meets the eye
    And some can only feel and hear;
A few see better in the night.

To some the distant scene is bright,
    The world to others seems to blear,
Yet all must try until they die
    To see things not as they appear
But as they are to inward sight.

PARADOX

Existence and Freedom—these
    Are terms of a paradox
That bringeth Reason to its knees,
    Keyless, at a locked box.

Freedom contradicteth Being—
    To be is never to be free;
Beyond the lock there is no seeing,
    And this perplexeth me.

THE BUBBLE

Creation might have been a bubble
    Blown and punctured in the void.
All the happiness and trouble,
All the building and the rubble,
All the garnered grain and stubble
    Came when Glory was destroyed.
Creation might have been a bubble
    Blown and punctured in the void.

A GOOD CIGAR

A good cigar with rich bouquet
    Can make an idle hour delicious;
With demi-tasse and Grand Marnier
A good cigar with rich bouquet
Asphyxiates a vast array
    Of troubles vicious and malicious;
A good cigar with rich bouquet
    Can make an idle hour delicious.

WILDERNESS PATH

No matter where the wilderness,
    Once the path is made
It guides the footsteps of the lost,
    The wanderer, the strayed.

Be careful when through wilderness
    You bravely fight your way,
Remember someone else may take
    The path you made today.

Be sure you read your compass well
    Before you venture on;
The step you take may guide some soul
    When you are dead and gone.

A PRIVATE MAN

A private man, I do quite well
And I don't give a hoot in hell
    To know what others say of me
    Or hear the retailed misery
Of townsfolk that the gossips tell.

I feel no right to breach the shell
Of privacy where freedoms dwell;
    I am, and I shall always be
            A private man.

The right to know may have the smell
Of droppings busybodies sell
    For gain or notoriety
    Ignoring all propriety
And when it does it should repel
            A private man.

FORBIDDEN DOOR

I have a locked and secret door
    Between my heart and brain;
Left open, everything goes through
    And then comes out again.

A secret door forevermore—
    It's really much less bother
To do the things I have to do
    On one side or the other.

Locked in or out, I'm not quite sure
    And so I hide the key
Each dreadful time that I pass through
    To keep my sanity.

EDGES

Whenever we encounter
    Something really new
We feel around the edges
    The way that babies do.

And if there aren't any
    It's pretty sure to be
Too big for us to handle
    Comprehensibly.

But when there are too many
    It's often just as true,
Confused by what we cope with,
    We do what babies do.

Our world, it seems, depends
    On edges that we find
With random reaching fingers,
    With gropings of the mind.

TIDDLY TINKER TOWN

They turn the inside out
    And turn the topside down—
Everything turns round-about
    In tiddly tinker town.

It brings tears to my eyes
    As juggler, jester, clown
That nothing can be otherwise
    In tiddly tinker town.

Here images deceive
    And those of great renown
Play ghastly games of make-believe
    In tiddly tinker town.

For innocence long gone
    Better laugh than frown—
Just watch the way they carry on
    In tiddly tinker town.

PONDERING ON PERSUASIONS

When I hear some folks converse
    As dedicated zealists
I often ponder which is worse,
    The dreamers or the realists.

When realists come face to face,
    When dreamer faces dreamer,
It's fun to see, as they embrace,
    Which is the loudest screamer.

But when the dreamer must oppose
    The realist, my ingenuity
Bids me flee and hold my nose
    From noxious incongruity.

So here I am, condemned to walk
    With folks gone to extremes,
Pondering, listening to their talk
    Of sticks and stones and dreams.

POLITICAL CORRECTNESS

It was an ultimatum
Quoting now verbatim—
    Be politically correct
    And no one should object
To such a smug and righteous paradigm.

It's delightfully linguistic
And correctly altruistic—
    It's only a suppression
    Of objectionable expression
And not the least bit harmful or fascistic.

Perhaps with paraphrasing
Censorial and amazing
    One can put in other words
    Of sonants, sneers and surds
All the niceties and nasties of dispraising.

THE BROAD CONSENSUS

To harvest opinion
The bean counters
Sample the fields
With selective fingers
Weighting their sacks
With rocks.

INTERVIEW

The loaded question
Fired into the heart
Seeks its target
Truth
Emerges
Ricochets
And wounds
The questioner.

DECADENT PURITANISM

Ah, to censor, sue and torment
    Neighbor, youngster, husband, wife!
Oh, what decadent excitement—
    Prelude to a stress-free life!

Self esteem and victim's rights,
    Pressure groups and laws passed
Make for peaceful days and nights—
    Sexless, speechless, unharassed!

Oh, such social, moral bliss!
    Conformity makes perfect sense.
Ah, to live a life like this—
    Snug in smug intolerance!

TALLYHO!

Plus and minus, equal sign,
    Are tricky tracks to follow
Chasing meaning and design
    Over hill and hollow.

The hunt in never-never land
    Breaks briar and branch asunder
For something more to understand
    Than simple awe and wonder.

The scentless symboled trail leads on—
    The hounds in full cry follow—
All is the same when they are gone
    Over hill and hollow.

AIR WAVES

Too many folks are tellin' us
    What we should think and do!
It's raisin' such a ruckus,
Such a mucky fuss and muss,
All we can do is churn and cuss,
    Simmer, sweat and stew.

It's a talky generation
    And they put their backs into it!
But it's hell and all tarnation,
Pit and fire of information,
Breakin' wind for our salvation
    Yet some folks have to do it.

We like as not could get along
    And somehow muddle through
Without them comin' on so strong
With what's so right and what's so wrong
And tellin' us where we belong,
    As if—as if they knew!

HOMONIDS

I've always liked the katydids
    And listen to their songs with glee,
And I have climbed the pyramids
    By reading Egyptology.

With katydids and pyramids
    I'm always quite at ease, you see,
But I'm distressed by homonids
    That function electronically.

Their ids are not like other ids,
    They're monstrous anatomically;
Their diode eyes that have no lids
    Send shivers down my family tree.

Watch, if you must, these homonids
    Play bits and bytes with silicon kids,
But I shall climb great pyramids
    And sing love songs with katydids.

PUBLIC LIFE

Before you venture out beware
    The dungeon with its moans and groans—
Inquisitors are everywhere
    With legal pads and microphones.

The Rule of Law has eyes and ears
    All licensed with the right to know
Both surface truth as it appears
    And dark truth lurking far below.

Beware the questions that contain
    The answers you are asked to give!
Your silences, should you abstain,
    Will brand you as a fugitive.

In public life, where words prevail,
    Be careful lest you learn too late
Some answers are of no avail
    And privacy may seal your fate.

INFORMATION HACKER

Forget the Necromancer!
    Forget the Holy Writ!
The Question is the Answer—
    The Bit is the It.

The Yes-or-No, though eerie,
    With strange finality
Is the Logic of the Query
    And It Reality.

Too bad that in the Question
    And Software of the It
Lurks a self-destruct suggestion
    Of the Byter bit.

NUMBERS

Ones and zeros
Marching, marching
Rank and file
On finite fields
To reach infinity.

The eyes
Weep with watching
Weep with counting
Ones and zeros
Without end.

WHATEVER HAPPENED TO ESPERANTO?

The towers of Babel touch the skies
    With satellites among the stars—
Myriad tongues wag truths and lies
    To Venus, Mercury and Mars.

The pandemonium of words
    Where dwell the demons of confusion
Makes parrots talk to mockingbirds
    With sounds of unrestrained profusion.

There is no common lexicon—
    No common language of mankind—
The babble just goes on and on,
    Vexatious to the ears and mind.

THE HYPOCHONDRIAC

He never had been really ill
    And yet to health he was a slave
        A vexed and peevish fretter.

To every nostrum, dose and pill
    Purveyed by charlatan and knave
        He was a doleful debtor.

And he was not content until
    He quacked himself into his grave
        By trying to feel better.

STARES

So many times
When people stare
It isn't there
Or anywhere

Unless it's where
The terrors hide
And dreams abide
Deep, deep inside.

THEN

Not yet, but soon
Not now, but when—
The then recedes
Beyond
The drawn and quartered moon.

The calendar's black fangs
Wait silently
To bite the heart
When least expected
Not now, but then.

THE UMBRELLA

Open, the Umbrella
Shelters all that's left
When it is closed again.

Closed, the Umbrella
Is waiting warp and weft
While warning clouds remain.

Lost, the Umbrella
Leaves heart and soul bereft
In time's hard falling rain.

HISTORY

It must have been grand
    When the world was new
And everything stupid
    Was still to do.

THE GURU

A mystic with infinite feeling
Brewed a strong pot of Darjeeling;
    He stirred it alone
    With a forked chicken bone
And poured it in cups on the ceiling.

FOOTNOTE

When all's said
And done
Kicking a few clods
Into one's own grave
Is a clarifying footnote.

THAT GRIZZLY BEAR

Nobody tellin' you what to do,
    Nobody pushin', nobody dare,
    Nobody askin', nobody care—
You don't want to,
You don't have to
    Fight that grizzly bear.

Nobody here to cheer you up,
    Nobody got a gun or chair,
    Nobody say it's your affair—
You don't want to,
You don't have to
    Fight that grizzly bear.

Nobody see when it's all through,
    Nobody pickin' up bones and hair,
    Nobody here or anywhere—
You don't want to,
You don't have to
    Fight that grizzly bear.

TOMORROWS

At night before I go to sleep
    My drowsy fancy gently strays
To little boxes where I keep
    Tomorrows of my yesterdays.

In secret drawers, in boxes small,
    Side by side in little trays,
I've marked the lot that these are all
    Eternals of my yesterdays.

I touch each one and would atone
    For all my foolish, temporal ways;
It comforts me that I have known
    The essence of my yesterdays.

Though I regret the lost and gone,
    Hope everlasting stays and stays—
A golden light that shines upon
    The meaning of my yesterdays.

And so I gently fall asleep
    With little drawers that hold the trays
Of little boxes where I keep
    Tomorrows of my yesterdays.

LIFE & DEATH

FANTASY

When fantasy no longer thrills
    The taste buds of emotion's tongue
Reality, with all its ills,
    Is bittersweet and life among
The creature things, the vales and hills,
    Recalls a time when we were young—

A time when every living thing
    Was clothed with magic all its own—
When every creature, foot and wing,
    Every leaf and flower and stone
Had something wonderful to bring
    To share, unasked, with us alone.

Now older grown, we seek again
    The purity of bliss we knew
Before our knowledge made us vain—
    Before the doubts, the false and true,
Made fantasy our flight from pain
    And youth and innocence were through.

THE CRUCIBLE

The incurable and the terrible,
    Each in its time and place,
Requires us to bear the unbearable
    In life and death's embrace—

To endure the unendurable
    That time can never erase—
To suffer as best we are able
    Steps we can never retrace.

This is the fiery crucible
    Smelting the fine from the base—
Reducing the irreducible
    Of patience, courage and grace.

VIEWPOINTS

This is just the way we are
And what we are:
    Rational, curious, changing change,
    Ordering as we rearrange
        The concrete with the pure abstract.
    Not to do so would be strange—
        How else should mortals think and act?
This is just the way we are—
    And that's a fact.

This is just the way we are
And what we are:
    Intuitive, intimate, feeling flow
    Directionless as afterglow,
        Feeling time immeasurably.
    It would be strange were it not so—
        How else should mortals feel and be?
This is just the way we are—
    Indubitably.

HALFWAY HOUSE

The halfway house of nature is my home
    Away from home; you might say, if you will,
I dwell in catacomb and hippodrome
    As one predestined for the chill and thrill
Of bones and groans and aerial acrobats,
    Calliopes and snickersnees and braid parades
Of fall-down clowns, white rabbits out of hats,
    Spun sugar plumes and requiem serenades.
Halfway between my earth-birth and my why-cry,
    Among my pots and pans, my balls and bowls,
Pale skeletons ride hippopotami
    And high-wire walkers rosin slippery soles.
The king of beasts pursues a wound-up mouse
Beneath the dome of this, my halfway house.

I AM LOOKING FOR WAYS

I am looking for ways youthful enough to heal
    Old wounds, and heedless enough to hurt again
What's left of me that's tender. I want to feel
    The God-forsaken loneliness of rain
At seventeen, the rumple of hot clothing,
    And the desperate ache for some improbable woman
Older and full of danger. I invite loathing
    Of all things moderate, mechanical and inhuman.

On the white sand of beaches, in crowded places,
    On piers, streets, busses—in the shared seat—
I search for the flint and tinder of young faces,
    Move to the hot rhythm of young feet,
Inviting fires that will leave my heart in flames:
Perfumes, red hair, and the sweet sound of names.

THE QUEST

How best to live and then how best to die
    Assail the questing spirit; how best to hold
Communion with all other lives and try
    To reach the depths unseen, the deep untold.

A life is real; its image, too, is real—
    An imitation of the thought to be;
Not the secret inmost life we feel
    But lensed and mirrored false reality.

The real is given; yet a life must find
    Its way as best it can with blood and breath
Among the myriad mirrors of the mind,
    The false reflected images of death.

The imaged universe of thought confounds
    The purity of spirit in its quest;
Bedeviled or deceived, the mind propounds
    Not what is real but only what is guessed.

CONSTRUCTS

Of all who walk the earth no two agree
On what it is they hear or touch or see.
    Each has his own contrivance to receive,
    His own inventive genius to conceive
The images that crowd his memory.

The fingerprint, the zebra stripe, the leaf,
The retina, unique beyond belief,
    Bespeak the Art of Nature to devise
    A world of recognition and surprise,
A realm of loneliness and private grief.

The constructs of the mind are Nature's way
Of courage to endure the dark dismay
    Of solitude and lonely doubt's persistence
    Throughout the troubled hours of brief existence.
With these we dream by night and watch by day.

FRAME OF DARKNESS

The last is like the first—we come, we go;
    The edge of darkness frames our instant spark
From iridescent burst to afterglow;
    We pass like stars from dark to cosmic dark.
Within the frame of darkness we must fly
    From edge to edge like fireflies in the night;
Our phosphorescence warms no ice-black sky,
    Our lantern is a cold uncertain light.
Our memoried passing keeps its tryst with time;
    Our afterimage holds the gone-before
Imprinted on the fleetingly sublime,
    Flickering in the dark forevermore.
We are but transient sparklers outward thrown
Like stars and fireflies through the dark unknown.

COUNTRY AFTERNOON

"To know how it feels!
        That's the whole thing!" he said.
"Swim bare-assed naked,
        stump toes, swear, get bee stung,
Hammer things, scream,
        eat grass, paint something red,
Put a rock through a window—
        feel wild, crazy and young!"

He rolled his own.
        "How soon we forget!" he said.
"We see and don't see,
        hear and don't hear; among
People who never got mule kicked
        or watched heifers bred
We forget how it was—
        to feel dumb, crazy and young!"

He scratched a match.
        "We sort of go dead," he said.
"We go with the green,
        stop with the red, get strung
Like fish on a stringer,
        all smart, but hooked in the head,
And we lose how it was—
        to feel free, crazy and young!"

He smoked and smiled.
        "It's the way we become," he said.
"When the good thing's gone,
        we're starved, not just underfed.
We all want to scream—
        run wild, get bare-assed hung
On a barbed wire fence—
        feel alive, crazy and young!"

ADRIFT

God Almighty, I am far from home!
    I am a stranger in a foreign land
    Where no one answers me or takes my hand
And I must go my aimless way alone.

I have forgotten how it was I came
    To be where I am lost, or why I cry
    For what was never mine, or why I try
To find someone who might have known my name.

Which would be sad, if love were not a song
    Remembered without words on lonely nights
    Made starless by the blinding city lights
Where strangers are and I do not belong.

God Almighty, I am far from home!
    It would be sad were not my song with me,
    Were not my home in all I touch and see—
Were I less loosely held and less alone.

RELEVANCY

What is pertinent to the case in hand
    Involves the texture of the universe
Of which we touch, sometimes, a single strand,
    A knot, a nexus, stubborn and perverse.

Devoid of history, world-time's mighty bells
    Strike uselessly upon the empty mind;
And life-time's wristwatch ticking only tells
    Of brief events, the now, the undesigned.

Our relevance, our glory, is how much
    We comprehend with reverent ideation;
The fabric of experience that we touch
    Is but the garment's hem of all creation.

PUZZLES

Our pleasures never last,
    Our pains go on forever;
There's something in the contrast
    Diabolically clever.

Our guilt and greed resist
    Analysis and ethic;
Circumstances seem to twist
    The abstract and pathetic.

That great things come from small
    Seems fairly sensible,
But to begin with what is All
    Is not quite comprehensible.

Our reasoning wants no truck
    With inconsistency,
Yet intuition, chance and luck
    Have strange persistency.

Our days are rife with strife,
    Bedeviled and befuzzled;
Confused, we wend our way through life,
    Loquaciously and puzzled.

EARTH MOTHER

Safe in her arms, she was our world,
    Our now and our forever,
Before our fingers reached and curled,
    Around the strange whatever.

How great the danger and the cost
    Of childhood's outstretched hand!
How sad it is, so much is lost
    In what we understand!

We cross our hearts and hope to die
    With all our sins confessed;
In myth and metaphor we cry
    Upon our mother's breast.

SOMETHING

There's something, always something,
    Felt, but undefined—
A pale, semantic specter
    On the staircase of the mind.

Unspecified, but definite—
    An indeterminate thing—
It haunts the unremembered
    That recollections bring.

It's a phantom and a vision
    To love or to abhor;
It's the ghostly apparition
    Of what was lived and died for.

It's the opposite of nothing
    That was lost when we moved in
To the haunted house of memory
    Where the ends of things begin.

BEWARE!

This day will nevermore return,
    Nor I, as I was before;
Accept me then for what I am
    Before I am no more.

Accept me as I am today—
    A bell lost in the sea,
A light that failed to light the way
    When storms broke over me.

This day will nevermore return,
    Nor I, from the depths of despair
Who cry through the tides and the darkness,
    Beware of the rocks! Beware!

BRIEF MEMOIR

We are a memory
    Of past things—
The flight path
    Of gone wings,
The spent wrath
    Of the left sea—
We are all that was to be.

We are what is yet to be—
    Our wings,
Our flight path,
    Our said things,
Our dark wrath
Are all there is of you and me—
Going—gone—a memory.

ILLUSIONS

How changed we are and yet how much the same!
    The world, too, has changed and yet remains
    Much as it was. Our boundaries and domains,
Shifted here and there, changed in name,
Are holding still, as in a radiant frame,
    Illusory structures that the mind retains
    To guide it through the maze that thought contains
As paths of darkness guide the moth to flame.
Between extremes of permanence and change
    Illusions of existence come and go
        Like moods of hope, indifference and despair.
When structures weaken, blur and disarrange,
    Like moths, we are consumed by what we know—
        Lured, until death, by what was never there.

PRAYERS AND WISHES

It has been said our answered prayers
    May punish us who pray
With consequential woes and cares
    That torment and dismay.

It well may be desires are stilled
    By laws that we must serve—
That when we have our wish fulfilled
    We get what we deserve.

Our prayers and wishes may entail
    Far more than we would choose;
Success may lie in how we fail,
    Our gain in what we lose.

Who knows what moves the Powers that be—
    What laws our Selves obey?
Who knows what shapes their destiny
    When mortals wish and pray?

IT'S ONLY LIFE

It's only life, don't let it bother you—
    It's only for a little while, you see.
It's something every traveler must go through—
It's only life, don't let it bother you;
It's just a little chore that we must do
    In booking passage to eternity.
It's only life, don't let it bother you—
    It's only for a little while, you see.

RAINDROPS

We fall like raindrops from the clouds of love
    Upon an ageless upturned graven face;
Electric passions in the storm above
    Make rivulets of fire, of time, of place—
    Like tears, we flow and glow and interlace
Along each furrowed line, each fissured groove.

Beneath the sun the wanton winds transform
    Our tears of life to mist. Our glow and flow
Evaporate, all intimate and warm
    Upon the graven face as we bestow
    All that we are, until—recalled—we go
To join again the rapture of the storm.

INTERVALS

Between the knowns and the unknowns,
    The daylight and the dark,
Are borderlines and twilight zones
    Ephemeral as the rainbow's arc
That fades in soft diminished tones
    And leaves no mark.

Between the present and the past,
    The faced, and still to face,
The lost and found, the first and last,
    Are mists of doubt that drift in space
To melt away when fear has passed
    And leave no trace.

Between the unreal and the real,
    The shadow and the shine,
What mortals think and what they feel
    In twilight zone, at borderline,
Are all the heartaches time will heal
    And leave no sign.

FORECAST

Before our moods and memories blur,
  This much we should foreknow:
In what we hasten or defer,
  In what we press for or forego,
We're much the same as what we were,
  Only now we're more so.

In what we keep or throw away,
  In how we lose or gain,
In when we choose to go or stay,
  Of what we most complain—
In all we wish and do and say
  Our tendencies remain.

Lighthearted, dreary—wit or bore—
  This much we should foreknow:
We're caught in a revolving door
  And where we've been we'll go
As self-set as we've been before,
  Only now we're more so.

CONFIDENTIALITY

A treasure beyond price the world around
  Despaired of by the old, scorned by the young,
The jewel of wisdom sought but never found
  Is when to speak and when to hold our tongue.
What to divulge, and what to self-contain?
  How much to tell when telling spells disgrace?
Will revelation compensate for pain?
  Who knows the truth of why, of time, of place?
The confidential bonds of mind and heart
  Once broken may release a flood of woe.
Who knows what secret worlds will fall apart,
  And who shall judge who has the right to know?
May silent mercy guard our tongue and thought
When we must speak but know not what we ought.

CHAIRMAN OF THE BOARD

Try not to get down to specifics with God—
    It simply won't do, don't you know;
It would be too unseemly running to God
    With a toothache or pain in the toe.

Pain is a policy, set at the top,
    As is pleasure, frustration and luck;
It's really quite sick not to know when to stop
    Complaining and passing the buck.

Love and forgiveness, endurance and fear
    Are guidelines, but hardly much more,
For if God had to personally wipe up each tear
    He'd be God with a rag on the floor.

And that wouldn't do; it's just not His job
    To handle each detail and flaw,
To pick up behind every slovenly slob—
    That's why He fills us with awe.

It's His works and His wonders, His over-all plan,
    That has our respect; it's the way
He keeps His hands off and trusts every man
    To mold or to mangle his clay.

SO MANY THINGS

There are so many things beyond recall
    Deep buried in the silent tomb of days;
On lonely nights their shrouded footsteps fall
    Like shadows through forbidden passageways.
There are so many things that must remain
    In rags and remnants, for the tomb alone;
Forgetfulness transmutes love's joy and pain
    To chambered echoes throbbing in the stone.
There are so many things the heart holds fast,
    Pursuing, helpless, as they drift away
Into the darkness of the buried past
    Where only vibrant stone and echoes stay.
On lonely nights, far from the light of dawn,
So many things, so many things, are gone.

ANXIETY OF MEANING

What do I lack that should seek
Another body, an aura, past lives, supersensory
Communication with stones, colors, crystals,
Stars, sounds of humming, of words, signs,
Silence, breathing, vibrations, numbers,
Pyramids, planets, unidentified flying objects,
Channels to otherness, healing, harmony, health,
Energy, light, ecstasy?
Why do I seek perfection, certainty, answers
From the unseen through meditation, mantras,
Trances, tarot cards, meridians,
Wheels, prayers, immolation?

Why is the pain of existence, being, mortality,
Incompleteness, so great that I must seek
Oneness, timelessness, self-abnegation,
Continuity, bliss, eternity?
What do I lack that I should seek
Unity, fulfillment, everlasting peace,
Unending blessedness, infinite love and grace,
When these are mine, already mine,
In spirit, heart and soul, conceiving, yielding
With body, mind and faith just as I am?

ETERNAL ARROWS, TIMELESS CLOCKS

It seems to me that time, as we grow old,
    Speeds up, as if our arrowed lives had found
An upper atmosphere grown thin and cold,
    As frictionless as mirrored sight and sound.
Our barbed and feathered shafts no longer find
    Familiar targets in the void of space
Between the clock hands of the heart and mind
    That pass and repass on the clock's still face.
Our faster flight from birth's abandoned bow
    Lies not within our power to guide or stay;
As days and nights fly by, it is as though
    Our gravitational ties were slipped away.
Directionless and motionless we fly
Borne on a stillness as we wait to die.

THE GLORY

All men see God, yet each one in his way
    Sees differently. Each has his time, his place,
His history and circumstance, his own dismay,
    His awe at what his thoughts embrace
In hours of reverence as from day to day
    He grows in goodness and in inward grace.
Each views in secret, silent and apart,
The wonder of God's glory in his heart.

All men see God, but not quite in the way
    One sees an object, set in time and place,
But as a sense of awe and deep dismay
    At life without the thought, the warm embrace
Of all pervasive love from day to day
    That is the human spirit's state of grace.
The wonder of God's glory is a part
Of all who are devout in mind and heart.

JUDGMENT

Life is precious, say we all,
    And precious, too, is liberty;
They must be kept whate'er befall,
    We must survive, we must be free.

Yet some there are who suffer pains
    Beyond the strength of flesh to bear;
And others who endure their chains,
    Too weak to fight, too tired to care.

Faced with judgment, who are we
    To say the struggle must not cease
When some in chains lie willingly
    And some in death seek quick release?

Let come what will, to each his own,
    And may his path be heaven blest;
Let each man go his way alone
    To find his freedom and his rest.

VAGABOND

I came into this world with nothing
    But a gambler's chance to survive,
And I've made the most of what I had
    In the struggle to stay alive.

The most wonderful things that have happened
    Were the ones I could never preserve;
I have loved all things that were insecure
    And the leaps that called for nerve.

I have loved when loving was useless
    And lived in a vagabond way;
I have traveled the weedgrown backroads
    Of time's lost yesterday.

My thoughts were the thoughts of a spendthrift
    With mind and spirit enraptured,
And I've lived in a clean world of freedom
    Where nothing is harmed or captured.

It's been good to be born unfettered
    And free in this walking Bastille—
To repudiate all that's material—
    To feel what the blessèd must feel.

So long as I live let me measure
    My days with the spade God gave;
Let me live with a scorn for treasure
    And rest in a pauper's grave.

PAIN

If nothing hurts there is no healing—
    Only dead men feel no pain.
Pain is life and love revealing—
If nothing hurts there is no healing.
Indifferent death is unappealing—
    Best to suffer and complain.
If nothing hurts there is no healing—
    Only dead men feel no pain.

SAD FELLOW

This morning I'm going
To practice my cello
And take a long walk
On Waikiki beach.

But I'm not really going
I'm just a sad fellow—
As lonely as chalk
Out of everyone's reach.

I know I'm not going
I don't have a cello
And I'll never walk
On Waikiki beach.

THIS LOVELY DAY

I will not plan this lovely day;
    I'll simply lean
Upon the wind and let my way
    Be unforeseen.

Today I'll careless be of all
    My ordered plans;
I'll take whatever may befall
    And fold my hands.

This lovely day shall be a gift
    I give my heart;
On timeless currents I shall drift
    Till day depart.

And when the dark shall come I'll be
    A sleeping stone,
Content that I did not foresee
    Where I'd be thrown.

OLD POET

Old man
Old brush
One hair
One drop of ink
One love
One hour
One poem
More.

BREAD

Eyes burning bright, he said, "I've sinned."
Turned out his empty pockets, grinned.
"See," he said,
"I gave it all—
I cast my bread
Beyond recall
Downstream with the goddamned wind."

He rubbed his hands and stood like stone,
A rebel soul, apart, alone.
"Perhaps I'll burn,"
He said at last.
"I'll never learn
To pray and cast
My bread, like some damned usurer's loan."

He turned to face the stream, fast flowing,
Swaying with the cold wind blowing,
Said to me,
"If this is bad,
So let it be—
It's all I had.
Stand near, my friend—we'll watch it going!"

FORMS

This gnarled and twisted root,
This stream-worn stone,
    This leafless tree
    Charcoaled above the snow,
This broken doll's head, cinders,
And this bone
    Blown bare and smooth, made clean
    By time's sweet flow,
Call to the fingers of the mind
To reach,
    To hold and feel and turn—
    To gently trace
The line, the grain—
To feel the weight of each
    Bright glory
    In its vast enfolding space.

The heart cries out to keep
What none can keep:
    The hands make tools for making,
    Yet the clay,
The colors and the sounds
Are less than sleep
    That makes a dream
    And waking takes away.
But still this root, this stone,
This leafless tree,
Doll's face and cindered bone
Are deep in me.

TOP SPINNING TIME

When there's no way of knowing
    What you should do,
Or knowing what's going
    To happen to you,
Wait while your universe
    Spins like a top;
When the wobble gets worse
    It will slow down and stop.

When it lies and malingers
    Inert on the floor,
With the string in your fingers
    Just wind it once more.
With a whistle and whine
    Tops must be spun
With thumb spit and heart twine
    In sorrow and fun.

EXILES

We number and we measure
    As best we can
The universe of treasure
    Found by man.

We seek the indivisible
    With all our might;
We search beyond the visible
    Realms of light.

We strive to find the context
    Of time and space
That yields the mind perplexed
    Symbolic grace.

We belong without belonging;
    In doubt we roam
Like exiles sick with longing
    Far from home.

We count and mark our going
    From egg to star
Returning, without knowing
    Where we are.

METAPHOR

It has been said, and so it well may be,
    Man's life is like a book, for we are prone
    To make analogies with what is known
And speak in riddles metaphorically.
We like to liken, that all eyes may see
    Our trend of thought, the way our weight is thrown
    Beyond the measure of our words alone
To storied distance lost in mystery.

The book begins, and ends as it began—
    A first word and a last word, nothing more,
While in between, the storied life of man
    Becomes a way, a slowly opening door,
A light, a flower, a bright unfolding fan,
    And when the book is closed, a metaphor.

GOLDEN FEATHER, GOLDEN EGG

Down the shadowed vista of the ages
    Floats a Golden Feather, there to lie
    Beside a Golden Egg, as symbols lie
    That fall upon the heart from yellowed pages
Preserved by hands that keep the words of sages—
    All precious gifts to ponder and to live by,
    And if occasion should demand, to die by
When dark misfortune nothing less assuages.

Beside the Gold Flamingo I shall rest,
    And near the Golden Goose of Æsop's fable
        I'll cry again with laughter in my throat.
With Golden Feathers I shall build my nest;
    With Golden Eggs I'll grace my Master's table,
        And this, my life, shall be an anecdote.

BUILD ME A BRIDGE

Build me a bridge, that I may bear my years
    From birth to death across the dangerous deep
Of ignorance, intolerance and fears
    In safety to the shore where I shall sleep.

    True soul-steel must the glorious structure keep
To stand the weight of strife and human tears;
Build me a bridge, that I may bear my years
    From birth to death across the dangerous deep.

No wind-blown rivets here, no joint that shears
    When heated logic's girders strain and creep;
Give me the best of minds—best engineers
    Of truth and beauty, scope, design and sweep—
Build me a bridge, that I may bear my years
    From birth to death across the dangerous deep.

BLISS

Do not be passive—inert—all receiving—
    Be not a slave to time and circumstance—
    But toward the vast Inevitable advance
As would a hero, purposed in his leaving
To seek the sacred grail of all believing—
    The cup of purity and heart's deliverance
    From imperfection, brevity and chance
In Reason's web of knowing and perceiving.
Beneath the gossamer barriers of cognition
    Lie deep unconquered realms beyond foreseeing
        Where dreams await in night's jeweled chrysalis
Their golden wings, rebirth, transfiguration.
    So must we wait, yet strive with all our being
        To touch the sacred grail, to find our bliss.

PRAYER FOR PRESERVATION

Preserve me now
Protect my inner self
Defend my heart and soul from vandals
Keep me safe from pride
In false perceptions
Of myself.

Preserve me now
That I may stay at peace
With what I am—let me pass
Unharmed through others' eyes
As if the looking glass were clear and I
Not imaged there.

Preserve me now
That I may stay secure
As stone within a stone—impervious
To worldly guile—preserve my inner self
Inviolate—unravished—keep me pure
This little while.

THE ASSOCIATIONS

After sunset when the world is dark
    The vast associations of the night
Proclaim the earthly sun a tiny spark
    In myriad constellations burning bright.

Each man against the world must seek his place
    Among associations less sublime—
Yet bear his instant spark with love and grace
    Into the all-enfolding night of time.

In contemplation when his spirit rests—
    When heaven blooms with starlight outward blown—
When constellations bare their flaming breasts
    No man on earth would challenge fate alone.

MISFORTUNES

Nothing can prepare us
    For ills as they befall;
Misfortunes of the present
    Overwhelm us all.

Immediacy of pain
    Defies philosophy;
The silent bridge of suffering
    Is crossed irrationally.

But then the past embraces
    All our grief and fears;
In sadness and remembrance
    The future dries our tears.

NOTHING YOU CAN SAY

The troubled heart
    The silent tongue
        The tears
        The aches, the fears
Are part
The bitter part
    Unsaid, unsung
    Of being young
    So very young.

But bitterer still
    The tears
        The silent tongue
        No longer young—
The will
The broken will
        That cries among
        The young
        The wounded young.

I MUST GO HOME

My glass is empty
    I'm empty too
I sit alone
    The thin dawn through.
The hours of plenty
    All have gone
The bottle broken
    The night done.

I must remember
    What I must know
Where I belonged
    A life ago
My street and house
    Before I moved
The last word spoken
    Whom I loved.

I must go home
    I must remember
Who I am
    Where I belong.

NOW AND THEN

The future we looked forward to
    And now look backward at
So often makes us wish we knew
    If this was really that.

We never are quite sure just how
    We saw it then and there
Because the way we see it now
    Has changed its when and where.

The now devours the there and then,
    The then, the now and here
But what might be—the hoped for when—
    Survives—if not too near.

STONES

In ceaseless dark, like falling rain, my tears
    Cry down upon the stones until they break.
    My worldly thoughts, so filled with life's heartache,
Grow bitter with the burden of my years.

My prison walls grow deeper with my fears,
    Yet, still I treasure all I would forsake;
In ceaseless dark, like falling rain, my tears
    Cry down upon the stones until they break.

I hear the echoes that the madman hears
    Who answers moans his inner voices make;
    As one in dreams who struggles to awake,
I clasp the night as terror disappears.
In ceaseless dark, like falling rain, my tears
    Cry down upon the stones until they break.

FUGITIVE

I'm running, running, running
    With covered ears and eyes—
A penitent in flight
    From appled paradise—

From printing, printing, printing
    I scan and throw away;
From pictures, pictures, pictures
    That flash but never stay—

From talking, talking, talking
    That dissipates in air;
From churning, churning, churning
    That goes on everywhere—

I'm running, running, running
    From all this appled fuss—
A penitent in flight
    To save myself from us.

PRECEPT

Be we wise or foolish-hearted
None can stop what we have started;
    What we do and what must be
    Have linkage to eternity
And never shall the chain be parted.

Conflict never will be ended—
Both offender and offended
    Are two goats upon one tether
    Bound to roam the world together,
Each in turn reviled, befriended.

Causal ties no man can sever—
Nothing helps him whatsoever;
    Though his deeds turn inside out,
    Upside down and round about,
What is done endures forever.

Nature gives to man this precept:
What is past he must accept
    But what comes after is his own,
    His added link, his gift alone,
And that is all man can expect.

THE STREAM

Unmindful where the fountain lies,
    The child with paper boat
Meditates with watchful eyes
    The stream that helps it float.

It is a stream of mystery
    That bears his self-made toy—
Their harmony, his eyes may see,
    A wrong rock could destroy.

From this alone his mind may learn
    To treasure life's endeavor—
With innocence his heart may yearn
    To float and flow forever.

SILENT BREAK

I love all things that chime
    In carillons and towers,
    In clocks that tell the hours;
I love right words that rhyme
    And notes that come to rest
    As two hearts, breast to breast,
Fulfilled in perfect time.

I loathe the things that crash
    On earth and in the air
    In wreckage and despair;
I loathe the things that smash,
    That crush and squash and grind
    The heart and soul and mind
To baseness and hog mash.

I love and loathe, yet hear
    A far more precious thing
    That only sound can bring;
I hear beyond my ear
    Each rhythmic silent break,
    Each quick, sweet breath things take
When Nothingness is near.

DISASTER

In every word, on every breeze,
In every noise, in every sneeze,
In every drop of falling rain,
In every heartbeat stopped by pain,
In every spark that flies amiss,
In every touch, in every kiss,
In every quake of earth and hand,
In every wave and grain of sand
Disaster lurks to spring on me
And crush my equanimity.

And yet I listen, speak and sneeze,
Set my sails in every breeze,

Kiss my loves, ignore my pain,
Build blazing fires, walk in the rain,
Quake and shake, extend my hand,
Build my house on shifting sand,
Keep my cool and do my thing
Free as a kite on broken string.
Disaster well may shatter me,
But not my soul's tranquility.

BAD ADVICE?

If you never give in
You ain't gonna sin
    But it's gonna be lonely
    When you and you only
Ain't been where us sinners have been.

If you flunk double-dares
With the little bewares
    Skin creepy and scary
    Bone risky and hairy
Your affairs will wind up as nightmares.

When you're grown up and aisled
Wall-papered and tiled
    It's Godawful certain
    You'll be itchy and hurtin'
And wish, as a child, you'd been wild.

TWILIGHT

One evening as the sky grew dark
    In twilight's fading glow
I met a man in memory park
    Who had no place to go.

We shared a bench along the walk
    Beneath the trees of thought,
Too somber for the words of talk
    Our lonely nearness sought.

At last he said into the night,
    "Who knows how it will end?
Who knows how God will set us right
    When we have lost our trend?"

"We and the world," I softly sighed,
    And after that we parted
Into the streets of homeless pride
    Where sleep the broken-hearted.

INTIMATIONS OF INTIMACY

What do I see when I see what I see
Beyond my looking, so intimately?
What seeing is this—what can this be
That troubles my mind and mystifies me?

What do I feel when I feel that I feel
More than my feelings can ever reveal?
What is there there that my feelings conceal
That feels so unreal deep under the real?

What do I know when I know that I know
More than my knowing can ever bestow?
What is this this that my mind must forego—
That is blissfully mine, yet troubles me so?

THE UNATTAINABLE

Do you ever have the notion
    That God is out to get you,
    Or is merely out to let you
Be dashed by your emotion?

When you have to fight dejection
    Do you hear Satanic laughter
    At the dreams that you are after
In a world of imperfection?

If you do, you're only sharing
    The human lot of living—
    Earthly cruel and unforgiving
Of desire and too much caring.

In our giving and receiving
    We mortals, in our fashion,
    Are the dupes of pride and passion
And the victims of believing.

Though hopes and dreams may shatter,
    Still must we keep on trying
    While the heart and soul are crying
It will not—may not—matter.

SCATTERGRAM

With the chalk line of your thought
    And the plumb bob of your heart
Drop a golden line from heaven
    And snap it for a start.

Now lay your spirit level straight
    Across the center line
And strike the horizontal
    In a scarlet cross design.

Then scribe a dark blue circle
    Of earthly stress and strife
Around the four quadrants
    Of the ages of your life.

Within this circle make a graph
    Of choices, hopes and fears—
Black line the deviations
    Of intentions, bliss and tears.

Your ethics and morality
    Your whole life through
Illuminate this scattergram—
    And what you see is you.

SECOND SIGHT

The transcendental unity of life
    Is, in the end, a gift that we receive
Through joy and sorrow, suffering and strife—
    Through all that we imagine and perceive.

This unity of being is a love
    Enfolded in the Self as in a seed
Enearthed to seek the rain, the sun above,
    The very stars, to satisfy its need.

With time it sends out sprout and root to grow
    Against the storm, the insect world, the shears

Of chance, misfortune, and the slow
    Encirclement of days, perhaps of years.

Until, at last, on leafy branch, a flower
    Unfolds from out its bud of destiny
To blossom with a beauty and a power
    Beyond the reach of lifetime's brevity.

The transcendental unity we share,
    Our love of life, our sense of Self, foreseeing
The Oneness of all things, is always there—
    God's gift of second sight into our being.

THE SEAMLESS VEIL

Being, consciousness and rapture—
    Perfect intimacy—
These are words that help me capture
    All there is of me.

I am, I think, I feel, I dwell
    In mortal synthesis—
But oh, there are no words to tell
    My love, my bliss!

I work, I strive, yet ever fail
    To breach life's mystery—
To lift with words the seamless veil
    Of immortality.

My love, my bliss, my very soul
    Cry out with every word—
But oh, the Voice that would console
    Perishes unheard.

Yet broken hearts, by sorrow stilled,
    Love silently—
As I, who mourn that what I willed
    Is not to be.

ONE NEVER KNOWS

One never knows quite what to do
When doing has been done—
One never knows if one is through
Or only just begun.

There's a for-the-moment neatness
That every ending brings—
There's a sneaky incompleteness
In all earthly things.

There's fleeting joy-and-sadness
In everything that blends
In a kind of cosmic madness
With change that never ends.

One never knows, nor should one care—
One stops and starts and goes;
Somehow, sometimes, one gets somewhere—
But where? One never knows.

FREE AT LAST

You can go anywhere
With a tranquil state of mind
If you don't much care
For what you leave behind.

You might go romancing
If you should feel that way
Or might just watch the dancing
In a questionable cafe.

You might go atraveling
On ships to foreign lands
And watch the world unraveling
In unfamiliar hands.

You might go to Bedlam
And be quite happy there—
If you don't give a tinker's damn
You can go anywhere.

INTIMATIONS OF MORTALITY

How ever would we do without
The whole wide world to think about—
    The great things astronomical,
    The small things anatomical
    And everything that's comical,
Awe-inspiring and devout?

How else would mortals get a firm
Mind grip on flea and pachyderm
    Were we not mathematical,
    Speculative, practical
    And sometimes near fanatical,
Traversing life from sperm to worm?

I rather think we do, indeed,
Seek more from life than what we need—
    Still, we must investigate
    The universe and meditate
    Quite rationally, the while we wait—
Vain creatures who but dream and bleed.

MATCH HEADS

On the knife edge of the moment
    The felt, the seen, the known
Are only tiny match heads
    We strike alone.

The flame that they throw outward
    Is lightning sublime
That leaps and streaks along
    The knife edge of time.

Each a flash against the darkness
    Illuminates the past
Through which we see the future
    While match heads last.

AUTUMN LEAF

I have been here a long time
Beside this vine
This leaf upon my hand
Its veins upon my veins
Its stem along the sinew
Of my wrist.

Its chemistry
Has turned the green to gold
The sunshine in its cells
Sweetened the grapes
It was a good year
With rain.

My hand is cold with age
Yet I feel
The sunshine on my skin
In my veins
Sipping the golden wine
Of a good year.

LES DÉBONNAIRES

Blesséd are they who laugh and love,
    The gay of heart, the singers
Who walk this earth with rose and glove,
    The revelers and bell ringers.

Blesséd are they who dance and dream,
    And ride in cabs at dawning
Across the bridge of time's blue stream
    Stone broke, and yawning.

ON A PARK BENCH

There is a Voice that sometimes comes to me
When other sounds have died upon the days;
It speaks, and all the useless twisted ways,
That I have gone become one way to Thee.
This autumn golden leaf upon my knee
Wind whirled to rest, how bright it stays!
Its tiny flame has leaped and set ablaze
A world of light, a candled treasury.

Like some small lyric thing, this fallen leaf
Holding the full crescendo of its song
Imprisoned in an aching throat too long
Pours out its rapture, glorious beyond belief.
Then sweeps the wind with sharp dust in its blast
And on the walk a stranger crunches past.

I TRUST YOU

I trust you, not for what you say
But for every wound and scar
You bear where nature had its way
To tell me what you really are.

The lines upon your hands and face,
Your posture as you sit and stand,
The words you write all leave a trace
That helps me know and understand.

Your voice tells more than you suspect,
Your eyes say more than words can tell;
Your every breath has my respect—
I trust you, for I know you well.

For this I love you more, not less—
With Nature's truths of trust I find
Deep love and trust and blessedness
To body, heart and soul and mind.

WINE STAINS

When imagination falters
    And memories grow dim
We do what we are doing
    By necessity or whim.

We follow ways familiar
    But finding nothing there
We do the unpredictable
    With accidental care.

So it happens at the table
    When glassware is upset—
When we leave upon white linen
    The wine stains of regret.

So it happens by a movement
    Of the tired heart and hand—
By the reaching and the trembling
    We alone can understand.

BEYOND MY WINDOW LEDGE, THE WORLD

Far above the glare of lights
    The stars of heaven shine;
The world is wide that lies beyond
    This little world of mine.

The ticking clock, the shaded lamp,
    Are very near to me;
But o'er my window ledge the world
    Leans whisperingly.

EYES

Oh, how I love to sit behind the span
Of my two eyes and drive them through the crowd,
Rough-shod, across the ice of slippery faces.
I love to brave a laugh that's harsh and loud,
And drive headlong and strong against the man
Who gives no quarter, but returns a proud
Disdainful look. There's danger in such faces
And it's thrilling to go driving through a crowd.

Sometimes a pair of eyes comes close to mine
And warms a certain coldness that I feel
About the heart when driving much alone.
It is a warmth that melts the icy seal
Of some inhuman winter—warmth of wine
And firelight, and the snug protecting feel
Of furry gloves. But eyes pass by, and stone
Laid close to stone withhold what they conceal.

THE KALEIDOSCOPE

Between desire and what desire may get
    We watch each other die;
In intervals of calm we sometimes let
    Our fancies question why
Time separates, and why our deep regret
    So often makes us cry.

Language, too, like time, seems to divide
    The meaning of all things;
Five thousand tongues reveal yet always hide
    The deeper truth speech brings,
That in its fragments meaning will abide
    As stone where lichen clings.

Kaleidoscopic are the things we share—
    Events and words all turn
As turns the hand of God, and nothing there
    Outlasts its brief sojourn.
With colored shards and mirrors, faith and prayer,
    We cry, we cling, we yearn.

ON LOOKING A GIFT HORSE IN THE MOUTH

The choice was not my own that I was born—
    In dark trimestered silent secrecy
I never dreamed, with tissue wrapper torn,
    That I should be the gift I am to me.
    Nor did I dream that this, my liberty,
Would leave me so alone and so forlorn—
    So individual, self-set, yet so free
To struggle, triumph, fail—to love, to mourn.

I am distressed by this new power to choose
    My private way—to make, to break, to bind—
To mesh with other lives, to keep or lose
    My very own—to close or change my mind.
        Yet with it all, perverse integrity
        Makes bearable this gift I am to me.

SELF CONTEMPLATION

A self that thinks about itself
    Is said to think "self-consciously."
The subject, "I," part man, part elf,
    Must "think" about the object, "me."

"Self-consciously" is how it's done—
    The adverb is quite troublesome.
My spirit part is full of fun—
    My earthly part is often glum.

And yet, I weep when spiritually
    I regard my earthly plight—
More often I laugh earthily
    And put my spirit part to flight.

Strange subject, "I," part man, part elf—
    I laugh with tears—I weep with glee
That Consciousness should need a self
    That It might think self-consciously.

MAKING MEMORIES

Making memories is our way
    With joy and in sorrow
To bridge today with yesterday
    And reach a dreamed tomorrow.

Childhood's copybook stays on,
    Its scribbled pages open
To innocence erased and gone
    Where pencil points were broken.

With years, remembrance of the past
    Returns our youthful yearning
For love of all that might outlast
    Time's reckless, careless burning.

On memory's bridge of sighs we find
    In strange, mysterious ways
Tomorrows that we left behind
    Among our yesterdays.

SHADOWS

All things are infinite to me:
Earth fragments of Eternity
    Adrift on cosmic winds that blow
    Awareness of the world I know
Across oblivion's boundless sea.

Myself adrift, I only see
Brief shadows of Reality
    But as the shadows come and go
        All things are infinite to me.

Myself a shadow, though I be
Ordained to drift eternally,
    Until I reach the Radiant Glow
    That casts my shadow here below
And I'm consumed in Ecstasy
        All things are infinite to me.

PITY

Pity is not for them who drift
Too close to shore,
Whom the freak waves lift
To the meager sands
With puckered, pale, discolored hands.
Pity is far too bitter a gift
To lay at their door.

Nor pity the one who no longer clings
To a branch that's dry,
Who would break his wings
In the dark of night
Attempting that sweet, forbidden flight
Into a heaven of beautiful things
Where no dreams die.

Pity is not for the ones who cast
The coward's choice
When the bugle's blast
And the roll of the drum
Conscript their souls for what may come.
When men prepare Death's red repast
All fools rejoice.

Pity is rather for men with eyes
Who will not see,
And for men grown wise
About nails in a shoe
While the last lies broken that shapes the new.
For the little minds that would tyrannize
Let pity be.

CHILDREN KNOW

Children know the way things are:
  That elephants live very slow
Like big balloons, and not a star
  Is where it was a wish ago—

That things go up but never fall
  Until the people want them to,
Yet people do not last at all
  The way that rocks and nutmegs do—

That milk pretends it's really cream
  And nothing ever seems to look
The way it does when it's a dream,
  Or talked about, or in a book—

That waiting for is not like hands
  Around a clock, or sand run through,
And memory-work's like rubber bands
  That break just when they oughtn't to—

That nothing's under leaves of fig
  Or on both sides of any wall,
And things alive are much too big
  And when they die they're much too small—

That similes and made-up names
  And metaphors and all such stuff
Are pretty good, and so are games
  Like hide-and-seek and blindman's buff.

LIFE WITHOUT FATHER

My mother married my father during the
season
For some unpublished, though probably natural
reason;
Then, learning to loathe each other, beak, bone,
and feather,
They began splitting worms and quit flying
together.

My father, I hear, was a bit of a singer and
spender,
Up with the sunrise and off on a cherry-juice
bender,
But Mother was close, saving string and always
complaining
Even on days when there wasn't a chance of it
raining.

Our nest grew shabby, the tree where we lived
unbearable;
Life without Father was bad; in fact, it was
terrible.
Mother grew hard, and one morning, asking God's
pardon,
She booted me over, head foremost, into the
garden.

I've never been back, and I've never been
homesick a minute;
The tree of my birth, I loathe it, and every
bird in it.
The world's full of cats, and my mother, I hear,
has remarried;
They live, so I'm told, just above where my
father is buried.

FATE IS FATE

Fate is Fate:
Fate has no rancor
Yet this sail
Is made an anchor.

Deep below
The wind and song
This weary heart
Is dragged along.

Fate is Fate
Yet I am ready
To hold fast
To hold steady.

This my lot:
Without rancor
To hold my ship
Secure at anchor.

BELFAST FUNERAL

The trouble and the change
Bring the songs
The tears
Handclasp and shoulder hug
The silent pledge.

The trouble and the change
Are lashing rain
Umbrellaed
In the storm
Far from home and doorway.

KEEPSAKES

These are my relic poems, the canceled checks
    Of all my life's expenditures of love,
    These words on paper, all spelled out above
My name. How strange that everyone expects
Some falsehood or some technical defects!
    A check might be a forgery and the sum
    Might be in error, only overcome
By writing out in full what doubt suspects.

How strange to see a date on love's affects,
    Receipted by acknowledgement of debt!
    I wonder, did the payee really get
The sum that only answering love collects?
    Endorsements, too, are sometimes false, and yet
Words from the heart are keepsakes time protects.

EXPECTATION

We live and love and die, the while expecting
    Things will be the same, yet not the same
    But variant with surprise, as in a game
Played brilliantly as we watch unsuspecting
Patterns lost beyond our recollecting.
    As forms are lost in clouds and dreams in flame,
    As gods are lost in time and pride in shame,
Soul patterns, too, are lost by our neglecting.
When life and love and death pass unremembered,
    Neglected, too, beyond our brief surmising,
        We will have lost the crux of all vexation.
When we, as fallen leaves by change Decembered,
    Arise unearthed to Springtime's sweet surprising
        We will have found our bliss of expectation.

THE LAST GIFT

My fingers close upon
    The void of memory;
They clench the loved, the gone,
    So desperately.

My heart will not release
    What is no longer;
My stiff hands find no peace
    In gripping stronger.

I tell my soul to yield
    What I am holding—
Release the loss concealed
    With palms unfolding.

Alone in my distress
    Tight fingers, one by one
Let go the emptiness
    Until it's done.

With palms outspread I lie
    Of all bereft,
Unclasped, beneath the sky
    With nothing left.

GOD, DESCARTES, ST. AUGUSTINE, PLOTINUS AND I

We are that point
Moving
Inconceivably fast
In an infinite number of directions
Simultaneously.

We are that circle
Whose center
Is everywhere
And whose circumference is
No where.

We go with God, with God
Alone
Into the Perfect
All Alone.

ANESTHESIA

Stone blind!
    Gone the last glow,
        shuttered the house, alone with fate
        in a black dungeon, there to wait
To find
    Which way things go.

No light!
    So intense
        The darkness, so cisterned the universe,
        so deep, nothing could be much worse
Than night,
    Night without sense.

Then dawn!
    So thin and gray,
        So tired against the wall, so weak,
        but there is pink upon her cheek,
And gone,
    Gone is the dark away.

THE LONG VIEW

How small one seems, how trivial are one's cares
  When, from the past, recorded history speaks
Of great catastrophes, and searching bares
  Lives long interred in vales, on mountain peaks.
How small the things, how few the artifacts
  The painted stones, the bones, the increments
Of life when hearts had wings to bridge the cracks
  Of ice and rock on shifting continents.
How small the earth, seen from a distant star
  That through the darkness shines within the mind
Upon the soul—and yet, how drawn we are
  To weigh the worth of dust we leave behind.
How small we are, how brave, in gathering gloom
To take the long view of impending doom.

THAT OTHER LIFE

So many streams I've forded shore to shore,
  So many fields I've crossed
To come again to where I lived before—
  But now I'm lost.

There is no marker, no familiar sign
  Of things I've pondered on—
Memories of the future that were mine
  Are lost and gone.

There is a bareness in the land and sky—
  An emptiness of dreams.
That other life, somehow, just passed me by—
  Or so it seems.

KNOWLEDGE AND FAITH

A vital radiance of life
  Glows in the atmosphere—
The universe of living things
  My love brings near
All tell my mind and heart and soul
  Why I am here.

For I am one with galaxies
  In cosmic afterglow—
With planet, star and nothingness
  In orbit I must go—
Myself a galaxy of dust—
  All this I know.

The force fields of my being hold
  My destiny—
With wave and particle I bear
  This life in me
To God in whom creation moves
  Eternally.

BEFORE I GO TO SLEEP

Before I go to sleep I cry
For all dear things that fade and die—
  My silent tears fall starlight bright
  Upon the pillow of the night
Where sorrow breathes its long last sigh.

Beyond my prayers, alone I lie—
With faith and reason, both, I try
  To still my heart from fight or flight
      Before I go to sleep.

Creation turns its breast and thigh
To tooth and blade as earth and sky
  Are ravished by the bloodshed blight
  Of weak and strong, of wrong and right.
In sorrow's lifeless arms I cry
            Before I go to sleep.

THE FOOL'S RHYME

Laugh with the king's son,
Weep with his slave,
But never tell ghouls
The place of your grave.

Never tell anyone
Where you are buried
Till silence and you
Are decently married.

And never uncover
A casual bone
To gnaw for the sake
Of gnawing alone.

Madness is refuge,
But ever uncertain.
Then keep enough wit
To dagger a curtain.

Laugh with the king's son,
Weep with his slave,
And hey nonney, damn you,
Get off my grave!

WOE IS ME!

The air I breathe is poisoned, so they say—
The food I eat could make me sick some day
And everything I like to drink well may
Both quench my thirst and take my life away.

I am the victim of the healing trade—
Insurance, drugs, and every aid purveyed
To market health where money can be made
From age and death and making me afraid.

The thoughts I think may do more harm than meat—
Cigars I smoke be worse than salt or sweet;
My fears are foes—too many to defeat—
Oh, woe is me who think, drink, breathe and eat!

A SPARKLING COIN

How shall I be old when I am old?
  What virtue shall be mine—
What beauty will this aged visage hold,
  What humor make these old eyes shine?

Shall I be tranquil when my years are few—
  Of what shall I complain?
Will I have many words, or just a few—
  With grace, from what shall I refrain?

Should thoughts become ridiculous with age
  And love be out of place
In this old heart, will untamed youthful rage
  Still flush this pale and wrinkled face?

With luck, I'll be, before my toes turn up—
  For just a little while—
A sparkling coin dropped in the monkey's cup
  To make the Organ Grinder smile.

THE CHOSEN

To be so chosen, yet not know for what—
To be foredoomed—no thanks, I'd rather not!
  And yet how else would all of us be here?
  Like small aquariumed fish, it would appear
That first we were selected, then were caught.

Between the hard place and the rock, begot
We know not why, like Abraham and Lot
  We must have trembled, must have felt quick fear
To be so chosen, yet not know for what.

Conception, birth, the severed cord, the knot
Have caught us all. But why are we so caught?
  And to what purpose? Nothing is made clear
  Until the end. And this I find quite queer—
That we are destined, fortunately or not,
To be so chosen, yet not know for what.

CIRCLES

Man's preoccupation with the stars,
Planets, supernovas and quasars
Seeks destiny in points and compass sweep
Inscribing circles, circling in the deep.

Past and present, future, would he read
In symboled light within the compass spread;
His curious mind, on pivot, weak and small,
Would scribe the greatest circle of them all.

Limitless, yet finite, sweeps the line
Beyond his power to measure or define;
His compass pricks are pinhole after pinhole,
A moving point self-centered in his soul.

Lost in thought, he moves among the stars,
Planets, supernovas and quasars;
His compass, circling circles, comprehends
Blank forms without beginnings, without ends.

The Absolute escapes the compass span
That folds at last, as folds the life of man,
Upon its pivot point, its start, its goal
Where all is as it is—uncircled—whole.

BEING OF SOUND MIND

I hired a man the other day
To come and cart my trash away—
He looked at me as if to say
    He thought there should be more.

It set my mind to wonder why
While we're alive and when we die
There's always someone standing by
    Who thinks there should be more.

Sometimes it seems that they believe
We're hiding something up our sleeve—
They judge us by the trash we leave
    And think there should be more.

I wonder—would it be unfair
To live a life so thin and spare
We left no leavings anywhere—
    Ah! Who could ask for more?

CARDS

To get and keep are hard—
Life makes it so—
But the hardest thing of all
Is to let go.
To discard the winning card,
To fold against the call,
These are hard, hard, hard
But the hardest thing of all
Is to let go.

Some card must be the last card—
Life makes it so—
But the hardest thing of all
Is to let go.
To fold without reward,
To watch the last card fall,
These are hard, hard, hard
But the hardest thing of all
Is to let go.

GOLDEN MOMENT

The flakes, the grains, the dust of fleeting bliss
    Escape the swirling pan beside the stream;
The tangled, threaded vein of happiness
    Is lost in rubble with the crumbling sea
    Time shatters in the darkness. Still, we dream
        With pick and shovel pain, and still we try
        For one great golden moment, by and by.

The shaft of hope, deep driven in the earth,
    Is tunneled through the rock of our despair;
The tailings of the heart that have no worth
    Are hazardous and barren everywhere
    That we have toiled. Crushed residue of care
        Is home to doubts the mind cannot deny:
        The scorpions of the when, the how, the why.

So goes the work. We seek eternal gold
    With paltry tools. Disheartened, we pursue
The endless shaft, maintain our slippery hold,
    Find failure at the end in all we do.
    But still, when life is done, the digging through,
        We yet may strike the Mother Lode, still try
        For one great golden moment, by and by.

THE DEBTOR'S PLEA

The magnitude of my indebtedness
    To God and Nature and my fellow man
Has overwhelmed me, and my blessedness
    Has left me bankrupt. I no longer can
Repay my creditors and debts I owe
    For food and lodging and the love I've known.
Through time I've watched my obligations grow
    And I have mortgaged everything I own.
I am a debtor fallen in arrears,
    Insolvent now, and helpless in my shame;
My partial payments made throughout the years
    Have never been enough to clear my name.
I seek the mercy of the Court and swear
My unpaid debts are more than I can bear.

THE SCROLL

Cathedrals of the soul
    And mansions of the mind
Are symbols on a scroll
    The spirit leaves behind.

The numbers on the clock face
    No longer tell the hour—
The fragrant depths of space
    Consume time's fatal flower.

The equal sign that contradicts
    All else is meaningless
As charm in old arithmetics
    And sums of nothingness.

The symbol for infinity
    Back-folded like a star
Is zero's final symmetry
    Where truth and beauty are.

And yet how great the scroll
    The spirit leaves behind
In cathedrals of the soul
    And mansions of the mind.

A TIMELY ADMONITION

Old age and childhood, people say,
    Should both be free from care
But both are burdens in their way
    That others have to share.

Both have beginnings in the past
    That neither could foreknow;
The end of each may come too fast
    Or it may come too slow.

Old age and childhood both explore
    And blend a memory
Of what has always been before
    With what is yet to be.

It is a precious time of life
    That sheds the purest tears
Before and after dry-eyed strife
    Of hardened middle years.

When burdens seem too hard to bear,
    Confused by love and rage,
Remember what it is you share
    With childhood and old age.

THE FUTURE

Our foolish hearts would have the future now
    Before its time, whose coming none can tell,
As if the blossoms on the springtime bough
    Could bear their fruit before their petals fell.

We seek the future much the way we dream,
    Outwitting time to have what cannot be;
Our dreams are raindrops flowing back upstream,
    Returning us from sleep's dark troubled sea.

We journey into lengthening shadows cast
    By what is now from what has been before;
The light, it seems, is always from the past,
    A flickering radiance of the nevermore.

Our raindrops blossom in the streams of sleep,
    Our shadows flow into the depths of night;
Our fallen petals drift across the deep,
    Forever lost on restless winds of light.

THE GIVEN

This little while I will not think
    So questioningly
But take what comes to me unsought
    More gracefully.

Nor will I seek the dark
    Of deep reality—
This little while I will not think
    So questioningly.

I will forego all myths and metaphors,
    All mystery—
Accept the given as if it were
    Sweet charity.

This little while I will not think
    So questioningly
But take what comes to me unsought
    More gracefully.

POSTLUDE

In solitude and starless night of calm,
    Eternal, all-forgetful, dreamless sleep;
    In endless darkness of the tranquil deep
There like the silent harp, the finished psalm,
    Where all things lie, the precious and the cheap,
    And what was I, and everything, all keep
The far quiescence of a blessèd realm.

All phantom joys, the illusory veil of pain
    Across existence flung, all earth desire,
        Are vanished in one long, enraptured breath
Breathed in but once and never breathed again,
    Breathed in so deeply he who would aspire
        To sweeter peace will find no kindlier death.

THE LOOM

From secret spools the threads of life
are spinning
The colors of a mystery sublime;
An endless wonderment without beginning
Blooms upon the boundless loom of time.

The living threads, the singing threads
are flowing
Thin and silken through eternal eyes
To weave a pattern beyond earthly knowing
Shadowed on the walls of paradise.

The broken threads, the fraying threads
wild flying
Are caught and mended by love's healing light;
The unspun rainbows of the soul are crying
Formless tears from spindles of the night.

The amaranthine flowers, imperishable
unfading
Rainbowed flowers of glory, full in bloom
Illuminate bright heaven's rich brocading
Spun from life on time's transcendent loom.

THE COMPANY

Within my limits I am free
To wish and wander aimlessly—
To be whatever I would be
Within my own identity,
My individuality.

Beyond my limits and my pride
There is no place for me to hide;
The world is dangerous and wide
And this is why I can't decide
To venture or abide inside.

The freedom that I have I'll lose—
I'll have to walk in others' shoes,
Endure the State and take abuse
And yet, somehow, I can't refuse
The promise of the power to choose.

Misgivings dire flood over me
As I forsake my privacy
And join the valiant company
Of all who once within were free
But now are bound in liberty.

FEVER

The fevered mind distraught invents
    Improbabilities from pain,
Twists space and time and circumvents
    The logic of the brain.

Distortion cloaks the unrevealed
    Disturbances life locked away;
Anxieties too long concealed
    Wear rags of yesterday.

The mind relives the shattered past,
    The hopes and fears, the yearning aches
Till heart and soul are bathed at last
    In sweat when fever breaks.

The insight of the hours reserved
    For images that hurt and heal,
Like sleep, in waking, is preserved
    Unreal within the real.

NIGHT-LIGHT ANXIETY

What image shall I fix my thoughts upon
    To bring me peace? What inner vision bears
The magic charm, when self-control is gone,
    To free me from a multitude of cares?

And what shall I perceive with inner sight
    That shall restore my self-command and calm
The storm and stress, the fight or flight,
    That locks my jaw and sweats upon my palm?

Shall I return to darkness screaming torn
    By knives of light that cut my life support?
Shall I repeat words learned since I was born—
    Tranquil words that comfort and exhort?

Green pastures and still waters beckon me;
    I tell my body to relax and rest;
A thousand mantras sweep my memory;
    A heart without desire slows in my breast.

Yet only when I yield and try no more
    A soundless whisper seems to cool my face,
As if a Presence passed my last locked door
    And touchless held me safe in its embrace.

PEACE RALLY

Full open throated love
Flows over me,
    One face among the thousands gathered here,
    One heart that sings with theirs the time is near
When justice will be done
And we'll be free.

Strong pulsing chords of hope
Sweep over me,
    Impassioned fingers drive the strings of song,
    It won't be long, my friends, it won't be long
When justice will be done
And we'll be free.

The whispering wind of love
Embraces me,
    A love that all the world can have and share,
    Pure love to keep our planet green and fair
When justice will be done
And we'll be free.

RELIGION

"I understand this dog," the old man said,
    "And he knows all he needs to know of me."
He stroked his hound's expectant, upturned head
    And looked into the brown eyes thoughtfully.

"We each know when it's time to go to bed—
    The time to wake, and go, and eat, and see
If we can do the tasks that lie ahead—
    And that's religion—come by naturally.

"It's in the hair and hide—it's just inbred—
    Nobody need agree or disagree—
Like when you're healthy, nothing need be said,
    And health is like religion, seems to me."

The old man broke the hound a piece of bread
And dipped his own piece in his mug of tea.
He stirred the fireplace embers deep and red
And laid the log to flame, quite silently.

SELF... SELF... SELF...

Let me be outside my Self
And see me not as others see me
But simply as my Self might see me—
As a Self that sees a Self—

Unpossessed of all appearance,
Being contemplating Being,
Unencumbered naked Being—
Substance me—not my appearance.

Other Self outside my Self,
What might you see of me in me?
What is this me that makes me me
Yet so divides us, Self from Self?

In you is there some Self-appearance
Unperceived, that has a Being
Just as my own Self has Being
Unperceived beneath appearance?

Detached, I am outside my Self
And touch myself; a Self inside me—
A kindred Being—answers me
With every heartbeat, Self to Self.

RESURRECTION

O sweet release from things my hands did set upon
And grasp too hard, too long! To find them gone
Is to have broken through, found swept away
The Night of Life

That once impenetrable gray
Mist, beneath whose ashen hands
The *Sturm und Drang* the shifting sands
Took place, is rent and torn.
I am the Risen Lord, myself pierced Death, been born.
Be still, my heart, be still. Have peace!

What now is mine
Bear not as I didst bear the Cross. Oh, bow not down
To Caesar now. This is the Throne of God; this the crown,
The Majesty, the Peace of Power. This is the Glory
And Reward of Death.

LINES FOR A FRIEND

Though understanding ravel out the thread
On which the difference hangs that men so fear,
Yet must we mourn, stand stiffly by our dead
Like blackened trees by nature rooted near
One tree that's burned. We felt the thin fire sear,
And when the sky-starved mouth of flame flowed red
We saw him fall. Oh, the trivial facts are clear:
The lightning struck; the breath of life is fled.

The flowers are bright, but brighter the tears we weep
When the way is closed and our going is at an end.
Though a kingdom's won, yet never was earth so deep
That it sheltered the need, the vacancy, left by a friend.
Our life is a fact, and death, but the heart's tight pain
Is a mound of darkness, and ashes pocked with rain.

THE SEARCH IS ENDED

At last I am to go!
They are waiting for me
In the white corridors of chemistry
With the incense of last things
And the empty promise of oblivion.
If they only knew the eagerness
Beneath my silence
It would surprise them.

Under the climbing roses
At the intersections of all things
I found nothing hidden,
Nothing at all.

In the Ark of the Covenant
In the highest of high places
In the Holy of Holies
In the *Sanctum Sanctorum*
Under all the front tables
There was nothing,
Nothing at all.

This has been
My lifelong sadness,
For I have opened
And I have searched,
But there was nothing,
Always nothing.

And now this, too,
May prove to be
Nothing,
Nothing at all.

THE SCARF

The old man sits upon the bench
    And sees the people come and go;
Wind-chilled, his gnarled fingers clench
    The cane knob of the long ago.

Beside him is a crumpled sack,
    The pigeons scatter from his knee,
His lifted hand would call them back
    With bread crumbs of a memory.

The people pass, the pigeons fly
    To safety on the wires above,
Bright-eyed, to watch an old man die
    In overcoat and scarf of love.

AWAY FROM THE PRESENT

I look to the future
With nostalgia
And to the past
With anticipation
Remembering my dreams
Of what was to be
Wondering what will come
Of what has been.

All has turned
Into its other—
Reality
Becoming its own becoming
Illusion
Lifting from the cold glass
Vanishing
As my breathing stops.

LOSS

The loss of anything may be the start
    Of woes that avalanche upon the breast—
The loss of some things surely break the heart
    Beyond believing it was for the best.
Yet, while the loss of some things may be borne
    If all the rest are better served that way,
Still will the heart in agony be torn
    That some must go while others have to stay.
When sorrow for the lost seems never through
    And Nature fails to comfort or console,
Perhaps it should be thought, and may be true—
    That loss is an illusion of the soul.
Perhaps all Nature, too, may be unreal
And sorrow more than earthly tears reveal.

GOING AWAY

For your journey through the cosmos
    When you plan your flight,
Take only what is needed—
    Travel light...travel light...

Perhaps a change of order—
    A memory or two—
A few sweet notes of harmony
    Will do...will do...

You're never coming back, you know—
    You'll have no new address—
And who's to blame you, if you
    Leave a mess...leave a mess...

At the airport one last whisper
    Will be your boarding call—
When your going casts no shadow
    On the wall...on the wall...

GOODBYE

We never know when we say goodbye
    How long goodbye will be—
    Sometimes we ask God carelessly
Our ways to bless and beautify.

But other times in grief we cry,
    God be with you mercifully!
We never know when we say goodbye
    How long goodbye will be.

With handshake, hug and kiss we try
    To make our love flow endlessly—
    But only God can truly see
The bliss our brief words signify.
We never know when we say goodbye
    How long goodbye will be.

A PASSING THOUGHT

I pray my passing shall not be
A nuisance to society.
Better far that I should lie
In Nature's arms and wait to die
Than linger in the cold embrace
Of cheerfulness that has no face.
Better never to be born
Than be so cared for, so forlorn.
Better far that all alone
I keep my dying for my own.

FALLING STAR

Life is a play toy,
    Not very strong—
Soon it is broken;
    Toys don't last long.

What will it be like
    When we go smash—
When we are broken
    Toys in the trash?

Who will remember,
    Who'll ever know—
What will the ashes
    Tell as they blow?

Death was a clean flame,
    Lovely and bright—
Like a star falling
    Down in the night.

LIFE AFTER DEATH

It's queer how people dwell upon
    A new life after death
That will begin when we have drawn
    Our final earthly breath.

Philosophers have said that we
    Are two extremes that meet
And death is like a legacy
    Our hearts spend beat by beat.

Our birth may not be what we say
    Or life what we go through
And we may never pass away
    The way we think we do.

It well may be we shouldn't mourn
    Or ever say goodbye
Since we may die as we are born
    And be born as we die.

I SHALL GO GENTLY

I will not show how much I cared and dared;
    I shall not tremble; I shall hold my tongue
    When I am called to take my place among
The undeserving and the ill-prepared.
With all the trifles of the heart I've shared,
    I'll stand as once I stood when I was young
    And hear again the songs I might have sung
On Helicon, before my soul despaired.
I shall go softly then into the dark
    As one who knew the glory of a flame
        More bright than all the stars in heaven's crown.
I shall go gently as a falling spark
    When in the night Oblivion calls my name
        And in my ashen bed I lay me down.

GAME

We see the traps and pitfalls
    Baited and prepared;
We hear the Hunter's false calls;
    We see how we'll be snared:
We all behave like animals
    Suspiciously and scared.

How cautiously we smell the bait
    And test the covered pit;
We hear the call and listening wait
    Before we answer it.
Yet in the end truth comes too late:
    We're caught, we're snared, we're hit.

We lie at last with root and stone
    And bleed away our pain;
Like animals, we might have known
    What now, in death, is plain:
The Hunter takes our flesh and bone
    And sets his traps again.

THERE COMES A TIME

There comes a time when everything
Wears out or fails or breaks—
When the heart no longer wants to sing
And every muscle aches.

There comes a time when laughter dies
On lips too tightly pressed—
When cheerful words are mostly lies
And silence seems the best.

There comes a time, and when it does,
Do nothing—only wait—
Possess your soul and all that was—
With grace accept your fate.

There comes a time of ended strife
Without a thought or care
Beyond the never-land of life,
The blindness of despair.

There comes a time, a better time
Than you have ever known—
It's just beyond the hill you climb
Defeated and alone.

IF DEATH SHOULD COME

If death should come, and hiding wait for me
To choose his hour and take me unawares,
He'll find me much as an old man, who, tired of smoking,
Knocks out his pipe, and slowly climbs the stairs.

DON'T SEND FLOWERS

embalmed today
after a sleepless night
my empty arteries
feel no pulsing urge
the aromatic oils
that stay me
from oblivion
grow faint

what I have been
dissolves away
as parchment skin
in silent galleries
of decay
embalmed am I
in linen coils
of time

a corpse am I
wrapped by the demiurge
as someone who somehow
ventured through
death's door
in dead of night
sleepless night
last night

THE INEVITABLE

The Inevitable is our common lot—
    Accomplish it we must,
But how and where and when are not
    Questions we can trust,
For, come what will, we know not what
    Awaits us, dust to dust.

The vicissitudes of life we face
    From birth to death may be
But earthly trials of time and place

Bechanced with joy and misery
To test if we can face with grace
Inevitable uncertainty.

The Inevitable may stretch beyond
The vastness of the sky—
A far Voice calls and we respond,
Never knowing why
Like starlight in a shallow pond
Inevitably, we die.

TO AN OLD FRIEND

A change of fortune came my way
And took me from the sea.
Sometimes I wonder what is there
That still remembers me.

Raw winds, high waves, a chilling fog,
A dead fish on the pier?
Or some old friend, like you, who waits
As I am waiting here

For things to change again and bring
The turn that sets us free
Forever from the need to know
If we remembered be.

THE ANGER OF OLD MEN

The anger of old men
Is a terrible anger.

In the folded hands on the cane
The finger on the pipe's cold ash
The eyes watching the clock
The early bedtime
In the old jest new to the young
The patient waiting
While others plan
In the soft food
There is no anger
Only survival
And the tedium of hours passing.

The anger is deeper
Gentler
Of an everlasting duration
Beyond the language
Of an old body
Beyond words
Beyond time.

The hot head
Of the burned out match
Sears the fingers of memory
And the mind drops
The unbearable
Hums long-forgotten
Song fragments
Everyone knew
But none knows now.

Listening to one's self
Is serious business
Breathing
Pulse
The rhythm of all things
The unrelenting destruction
Of change

The ongoing ceaseless wind
Blowing
Dead leaves
Old papers
Relics
The plunder
Of autumn.

The preparation for change
The leaving
The still beauty
Of all things gone
The vanishing
Of the undone
The unsaid
The might-have-beens
The sunlight
Passing to shadow
The evaporation
Of sweat
Tears
Blood
The hardening
The listening
In the night
Are all serious business.

Last transactions
Take care of nothing
For what is Willed
Is nothing
And what is left
Is everything
For who shall witness
What mattered most
And who shall distribute
The unpossessed
To whom the legacy
Of love
What codicil can cover
The after-thoughts
Of guilt?

Helplessness
Pervades all else
No longer prayer
In work
No longer faith
In making
Hands too weak to hold
The tools of worship
Fold upon the air
Like settled wings
And answers come unbidden
To unasked questions
Too deep
For talk.

Who understands the lifted hand
That says
Nothing is wanted
Who knows the meaning
Of closed eyelids
And who can share
The emptiness
Of words unspoken
That no longer matter?

The terrible anger of old men
Is the pain of being
And not being
And being again
The other side
The shadowed side
The whimper
Before the ecstasy
The last passion
Of regret
Before
Forgetting.

DESPERATION

When marked for death by circumstance
    Desperate men do desperate deeds
    To satisfy their dying needs
As days of suffering advance.

When they are looked at with askance
    In loneliness their terror feeds
On every hope and every chance—
    Desperate men do desperate deeds.

They call to heaven's wide expanse
    As Nature's frailest, broken reeds—
    They cry to every heart that bleeds
For their support and maintenance.
When marked for death by circumstance
    Desperate men do desperate deeds.

THE YOUNG WILL UNDERSTAND

We idolize the dead
    Who died too young—
We mourn their words unsaid
    Their songs unsung.

We flower their graves with tears
    And we enshrine
The remnants of their years
    As things divine.

We are the young of heart
    In death's embrace
Who feel, beyond, in Art
    God's love, God's Grace.

Scorn not our only way
    To take and share
As on each lonely day
    We show we care.

WAIT

Spread the white cloth on the table,
    Smooth out the rug on the floor;
Be patient as long as you're able—
    Wait for the knock at the door.

Pour the red wine in the glasses,
    Draw up the chairs as before;
Watch as the time slowly passes—
    Wait for the knock at the door.

Wait in the dark of your yearning,
    Build up the fire once more;
Kneel with the flames and the burning—
    Wait for the knock at the door.

Wait with a faith never ending,
    Wait as you've waited before;
Wait for the Bright Wings descending—
    Wait for the knock at the door.

GARBAGE IN GARBAGE OUT

Do the things you have to do,
    Say the things you have to say,
    Keep it up the same old way,
Be a robot through and through.

Take the pulses of your heart,
    Take your pressure every day,
    Then when you are old and gray,
Mechanically, just fall apart.

When the cleanup crew comes through,
    Sweeping where the pieces lay,
    They will haul them all away
And never know that they were you.

THE IRIDESCENT BOND

Be quiet, oh my soul,
    My mirrored self,
Eyes burning bright
    With love of life today!
This yours and mine
    Will here forever stay—
A time-reflected light,
    A spark divine,
An iridescent bond,
    Part self,
    Part soul.

Be patient, oh my soul,
    My imaged self!
One shattering blow
    And I alone remain—
A withered rose,
    A scar of vanished pain.
Then shall I know
    Release the giver knows
Who gives beyond
    His self,
    His very soul.

LAST POEM

I pause
The noise of going on
Is too great
The journey's end
Too near.

MAGIC MANTRA

Let me say the words to guide me
    To a timeless placeless nowhere,
Far from all the ache inside me,
    Far from struggle and from care;
Magic words to help me hide me
    In the empty everywhere.

Let me now no longer be me;
    Here I would no longer stay;
Let me go where none may see me
    Fail to fight or run away;
Magic mantra, gently free me
    From the torment of today.

Let me drift where nothing holds me,
    Far beyond all I desire;
Drift where Self no more enfolds me,
    Drift like smoke above the pyre;
Drift where God alone beholds me
    Lifting, drifting—higher—higher—

THE WILL

The will to live, the will to die,
    Is something wise men ponder on
At bedsides when, in vain, they try
    To hold fast to the almost gone.

The will to power, the will to yield,
    Tear love and loyalty apart
When flag and cross and battlefield
    All fail the wounded mind and heart.

The freedom of the will to choose
    Within the reach of self control,
To live or die, to win or lose,
    Exalts and vindicates the soul.

Though all our hopes be unfulfilled
    And freedom vanish with our breath,
Still must we be what we have willed,
    Or perish, overwhelmed by death.

NOVEMBER TWILIGHT

There is a time when it makes sense
    Just to wait—
To let the papers all pile up—
    The dust collect—
To let the yard stay deep in leaves—
    It is too late
        To welcome or reject
What lies beyond the broken fence
    The sagging gate.

It is a time to wait inside
    Windows gray
Where sill-spread nets of spider web
    Catch useless things—
Some by day and some by night
    That fall their way
        On spent, light-shattered wings—
It is the time one must decide
    To go or stay.

THE TRELLIS

A groping vine, I twist and twine
    Through latticed life's interstices—
    Sun beckoned in the fitful breeze
I climb without design.

I know not why I upward strive
    To reach I know not what—or even
    Why I clasp these rungs of heaven
Just to stay alive.

When tendrils shrink in winter sun—
    When latticework is cold for clasping,
    Death will scribe the everlasting
Climbing I have done.

With winding line of twining vine
    Through latticed life's interstices
    May be inscribed such words as these—
This trellis once was mine.

THE MARKER

My headstone should be small,
  A pebble well might do—
Throw it anywhere at all
  The fancy pleases you—

Perhaps into a deep well,
  Perhaps a looking-glass—
With pebbles you can never tell
  What may come to pass.

But if you're so inclined,
  Just throw it anywhere—
Out of sight and out of mind—
  I'll be waiting there.

SHIP'S LOG—LAST ENTRY

The storm has struck—
  My foundering ship is lost.
    Every stay is wind wrenched from my grasp—
    To my breast all my loves I clasp
With fear and hope,
  My heart and fingers crossed.
How wild the sea!
  How great the voyage cost!
    Above the storm I feel the dreaded gasp
    Of death itself—the heaving groan and rasp
Of keel upon the rocks.
            Tempest tossed—
Last entry now—
    My wheelhouse lantern throws
      Its dying glow no farther than my hand
Against the starless darkness,
            the sea's might.
Still, where my Compass points
  Upon the Rose
    I strive to see my harbor and my homeland
Beyond the storm—beyond
            this perilous night.

Index of Titles

HIGHLIGHTS OF KINGSLEY TUFTS' LIFE

Born on a farm in New Albany, Indiana, April 19, 1907.
Went to a one-room school through sixth grade.
Graduated from New Albany High School.
Graduated from New Albany Business College.
Pitched a no-hit, no-run game in semi-pro baseball and was offered a berth with the Chicago Cubs. No dice.
Bummed throughout the eastern United States for eight months.
B.A. degree in economics from Stanford, 1928.
C.P.A. certificate, 1928.
Worked for Arthur Anderson and Price Waterhouse in New York, 1929–1933.
Married Kate Frost, 1933.
The two were university bums, 1933–1937.
M.A. degree in Philosophy from Stanford, 1937.
Settled in Santa Monica, California, and started writing plays, poems and fiction.
During World War II worked as executive in shipyards.
Sold first story to *Saturday Evening Post,* 1946.
Wrote fiction and poetry for leading magazines (*Saturday Evening Post, The New Yorker, Ladies' Home Journal, Collier's, Liberty, Esquire,* etc.) 1946–1958.
During the sixties, seventies and eighties, went back to his first love, poetry.
Died Christmas Day while reading a poem to some friends, 1991.

In 1993 Kingsley Tufts' widow, Kate Tufts, established the annual Kingsley Tufts Poetry Award, which is administered by the Claremont Graduate School. The purpose of this prize is to give one poet each year a little recognition and the freedom to write without economic hardship.